Carving Adventure Caricatures

by
Jim Maxwell

Box 7948
Lancaster, Pennsylvania
17604

© 1994 by Fox Chapel Publishing

Publisher: Alan Giagnocavo
Project Editor: Ayleen Stellhorn

ISBN # 1-56523-051-5

Photography: Cover Photography - VMI Productions, Leola, PA

"Swiss Made" Carving Tools chart and photograph on page 111 courtesy of Woodcraft Supply, Parkersburg, West Virginia, 26102

To order your copy of this book,
please send check or money order
for cover price plus $2.50 to:
Fox Chapel Book Orders
Box 7948
Lancaster, PA 17604-7948

Try your favorite book supplier first!

This opera house, built in the 1890s, later became the movie theater in my hometown of Windsor, Missouri. Its auditorium was once filled with cheers and laughter and the smell of fresh popcorn as villains and heroes fought it out in action-packed adventure films. A victim of progress, its colorful marquee and projectors have given way to the changing times.

Table of Contents

Foreword

Watching old movies has been one of my favorite forms of entertainment since I was a young boy. I especially enjoy the movies filmed in the 1930s, 1940s and 1950s. During this time period, Hollywood created some very interesting and unique movie characters. Heroes were really heroes, and it was easy to tell who the bad guys were.

Throughout this book, I have taken many of the ideas and costumes used in creating these movie characters and applied them to my woodcarvings. The result is a host of wooden caricatures that appear new and fresh yet still bear a nostalgic resemblance to the old-time inspirational heroes of the Silver Screen.

Jim Maxwell

The projects in this book are all figments of my imagination and were designed for the enjoyment of woodcarving. They are not meant to be a likeness of any actual person or persons living or dead, and if any similarities appear, it is purely coincidental.

Jim Maxwell's shop in Cole Camp, Missouri.

How To Use This Book

To get the most out of this book, let's pretend for a moment that we are living during the Silver Screen era and that we are attending a Saturday matinee movie at the old Windsor Theater. As we watch the movie, let's see if we can use some of Hollywood's ideas to create some new woodcarving caricatures. We'll treat ourselves to a soft drink, grab our tools, and pick up a piece of choice basswood. It's almost curtain time, so let's get ready.

We will begin with a newsreel keeping us up to date on the war in Europe and the Pacific. You'll find a pattern and a step-by-step carving demonstration for a beginner project, Pappy, one of our heroes abroad. Next, we will enjoy a cartoon and previews of coming attractions, followed by today's serial chapter and a selected short. These smaller projects will help to prepare you for our Feature Presentation.

The Feature Presentation is a movie called *Ambush,* starring Broncho Buddy. You'll find a pattern for Broncho Buddy and another step-by-step carving demonstration for this project. Halfway through, we'll take a break during the intermission to stretch our legs and sharpen our tools. Then we'll finish Broncho, right down to his sharp-shooting rifle. We'll end up our day at the movies with a late show.

You can go on to create other movie caricatures with the ideas presented in the chapter entitled "Top Ten Favorite Movies." Here you'll find patterns for ten other movie caricatures, plus a third step-by-step carving demonstration.

Enjoy your day at the movies!

Movie Time News

PAPPY

DOG FACE

Today's newsreel will feature an interview with two American servicemen, Pappy and Dog Face. Pappy is dressed from head to toe in his sailor-best. He is ready to spend a well-deserved weekend out on the town and will be telling us all about the weekend pass. Dog Face will be taking time out from his many duties to tell us about army chow.

PAPPY is a fun project and quick to carve. His small size makes him comfortable to hold. By using the same blank and changing his face, you can create an entire crew.

Carving Adventure Caricatures

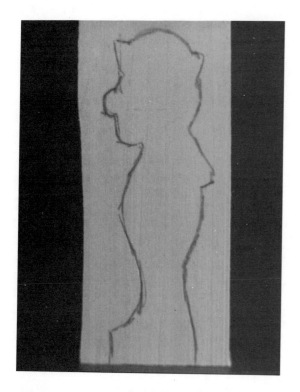

1 Start with a block of basswood, 2" x 2" x 4". Using tracing paper and a pencil, trace Pappy's pattern from page 2. Carefully, use scissors to cut out the pattern. Lay the side view on the block of wood and trace around the pattern with a dark pencil leaving a strong outline.

2 Using a band saw, carefully saw out the side profile.

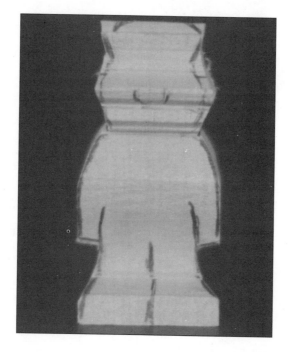

3 Draw the front view onto the blank and remove the extra material along the sides of the figure with a bandsaw. Make sure the grain of the wood is running vertically.

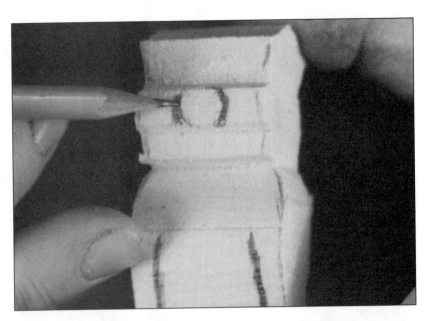

4 Use a pen or pencil to make a strong outline of the nose. Avoid using a marker or pen to outline cuts; ink is permanent and soaks into the wood. Note that the nose is an oval, not a circle.

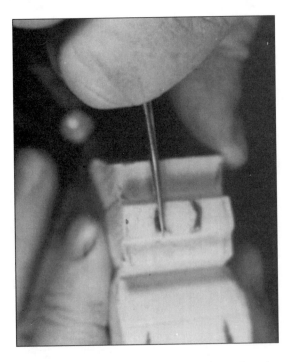

5 Using a knife, make a stop cut on the outline of the nose. Be sure to cut only a little bit at a time to avoid cutting too deep.

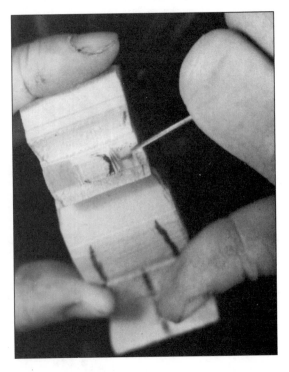

6 Continue to use a knife to remove wood from each side of the nose.

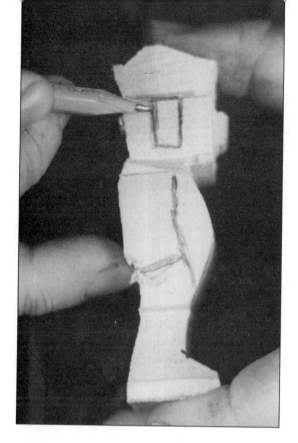

7 Outline the sailor's ears and arms. Be sure to position the ears correctly. The center of the ear and the center of the nose are on the same line.

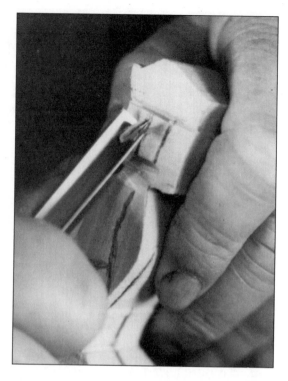

8 Use a large v-tool to block out the ears. Take the wood off in slow, deliberate cuts to avoid removing too much wood.

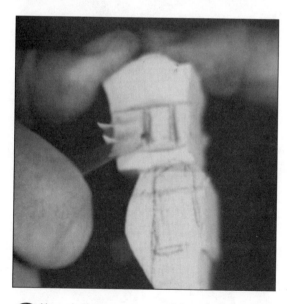

9 Use a knife to remove wood from the side of the head. Remember to use stop cuts before making the cut to remove the wood. Stop cuts will keep your cuts clean.

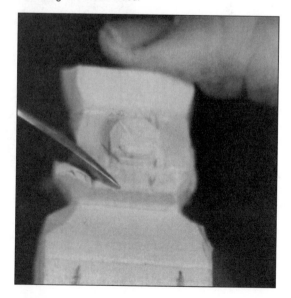

10 Using a woodcarving knife, round the nose to its oval shape and point the chin. You can also start to notch the neck at this stage.

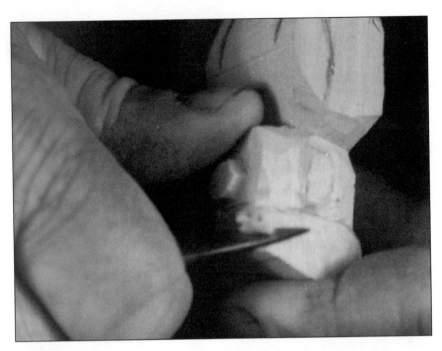

11 Round the corners of the hat with a woodcarving knife. The center of the hat is raised; the brim is concave. Note how Jim holds the piece upside-down as he works on this area.

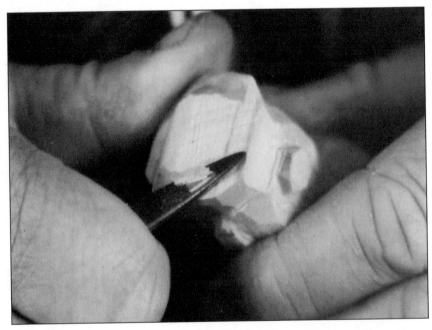

12 Next, shape the crown of the hat. Because you're cutting across the grain of the wood, you'll need a very sharp knife. A dull knife will cause the wood to fuzz.

Carving Adventure Caricatures

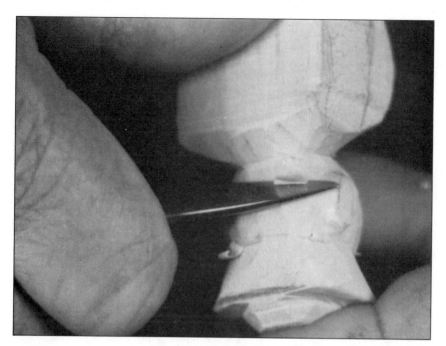

13 Still using a woodcarving knife, finish notching in the neck and clean up the shoulders. Shape the back of the head.

14 The sailor's head is now ready for more detail. At this point, check the alignment of the ears and the nose. Do any touch-up trimming to make sure the features are in their correct positions.

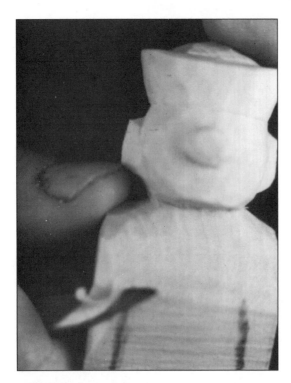

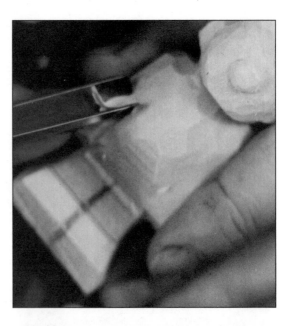

16 Use a large v-tool to block the front of the arms. The shoulders are narrow at the top and taper inward.

15 Remove wood from the shoulders and begin shaping the arms. Use a knife or gouge to make shallow indents in the upper arms.

17 Use a v-tool to block out the back of the arms. The shoulders line up with the neck and taper slightly inward.

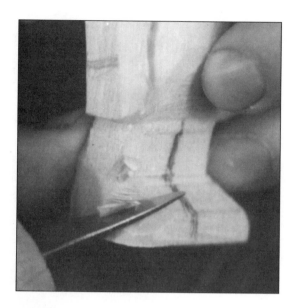

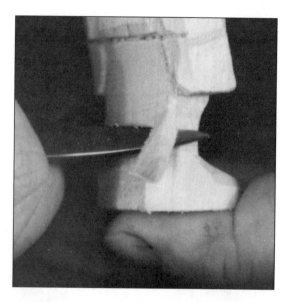

18 Use a knife to round the front of the feet and the legs. Remember, both feet are not shaped the same. Make sure you are carving one left foot and one right foot.

19 Next, round the back of the legs and the back of the heels. Don't try to make your cuts too big. Two small cuts are just as effective as one large cut.

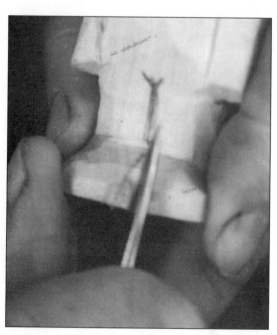

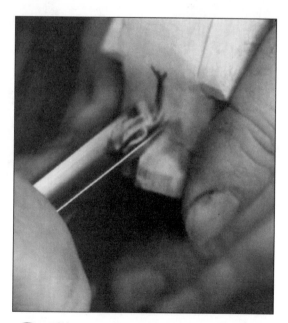

20 Cut a notch between the two feet. Be careful not to make the notch too big. The notch should be just big enough to put some space between the front of the shoes.

21 Use a v-tool to make a groove between the legs, both on the front of the sailor and on the back. Do not cut completely through the wood; it is not necessary to separate the legs entirely.

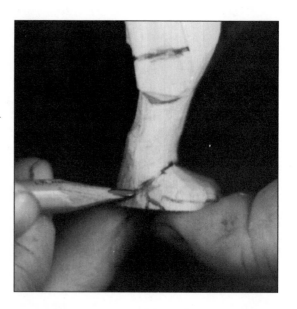

23 Mark the shirt cuffs and pant cuffs with a pencil. Use a woodcarving knife to make stop cuts on these lines.

22 At this point, the legs, feet and arms are all nicely shaped. Check again to make sure that the sailor's parts are proportional. Are both arms the same length? Are both feet the same width? Does your sailor have one right foot and one left foot?

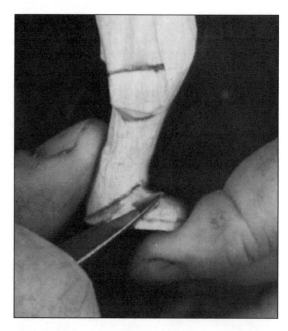

24 Remove the wood from the top of the shoes, cutting toward the stop cut to make the pant cuffs. Round the top of the shoes. Note that the top of the foot is curved upward above the instep; don't just make a square cut.

Carving Adventure Caricatures

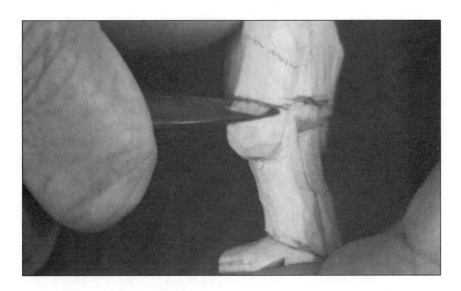

25 Use a woodcarving knife to remove wood from the wrist. Cut toward the stop cut to make the shirt cuffs. Be careful not to make the wrists too small; they should be slightly larger than the hands. Both wrists should be the same thickness.

26 Outline the thumbs. A figure this size need not have actual fingers; a mitten-shaped hand will work just fine.

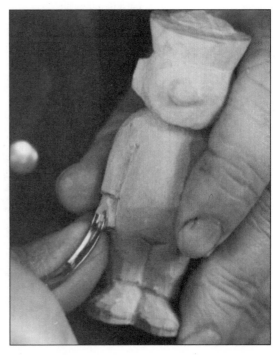

27 Use a small v-tool to block out the thumbs. Make your first cut alongside the thumb. The second cut should be made along the bottom. Finally, round the thumbs with a carving knife.

28 Draw in the outline of the necktie. It is not necessary to carve the detail on the knot in a figure this small. Also draw in the bottom of the shirt on the front and the back of the sailor.

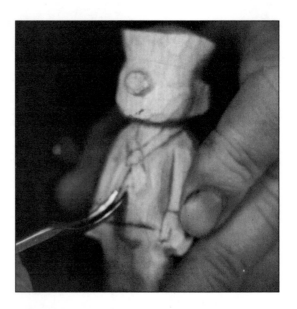

29 Outline the necktie and the knot with a small v-tool.

30 Remove wood from around the necktie so that it stands out from the shirt about 1/8". Also remove the wood from the area under the front of the chin between the two sections of the necktie.

31 Use a large v-tool to make wrinkles in the sailor's clothing. These wrinkles should be placed at random at the bend of the elbows and at the bend of the knees.

32 Use a pencil to draw on the eyes, mouth and hair. To make the eyes easy, I have drawn happy eyes that are squinted and arch up.

33 Use a small v-tool to shape the cheeks and mouth.

34 Use a knife to remove the wood below the cheeks and along the side of the chin. Then shape the sharp corners of the mouth. When carving a happy mouth, I usually set the corners of the mouth in deeper to give additional curvature to the tongue.

35 Use a small gouge to make a cut between the bottom lip and the chin.

36 Using a small v-tool, make a single cut to create the happy eyes.

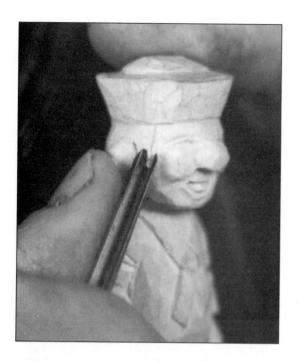

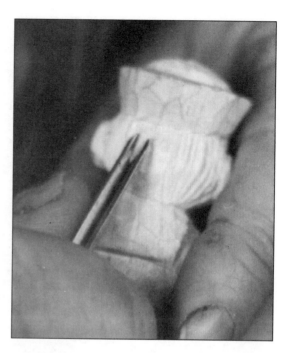

37 Outline the strands of hair with a small v-tool. These outline cuts should be very shallow.

38 Texture the hair with a small v-tool. Use randomly placed cuts, some deep and some shallow, to give the appearance of locks of hair.

39 Use a small gouge to hollow out the ears. On a figure this small, it is not necessary to include a lot of detail inside the ear.

40 At this point, it is very important to sharpen your knife and wash your hands and carve away all the dirt and pencil marks left on your carving. Dirt and pencil marks will sometimes show through the paint. I don't sand my carvings before I paint them. I feel I get a better "caricature" look if I leave the carving a bit rough.

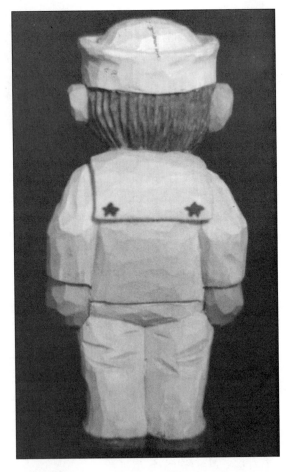

41 The finished carving is now ready to be painted. When I paint my carvings, I use acrylic water-based paints. I thin all colors a great deal, except white and flesh. I usually paint stripes, stars and insignias on these smaller figures. My real Pappy wore a propeller on his sleeve.

Carving Adventure Caricatures

42 When the paint has dried, apply a thin coat of toner consisting of linseed oil, with a small amount of burnt umber oil color.

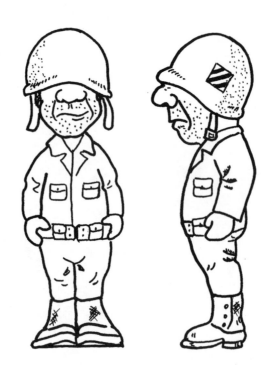

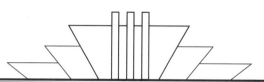

Today's Cartoon

The Voyager

You will have lots of fun with this one. Let's join our little friend traveling off in his long ship in search of new conquests. A long beard and bushy mustache obscure most of his face. A fur coat and fur-lined boots will help to keep him warm in his travels.

THE VOYAGER is wearing leather leggings that crisscross and tie with rawhide strips. His right hand is hidden behind his shield. By drilling a whole in his left hand, a sword can be added for more detail. Large rivets can be effectively made on his metal helmet and shield by using a 2mm gouge. The fur texture on a figure this size can best be achieved by using a 2mm gouge.

When painting the fur texture, use a medium-gray paint and highlight with shades of dark gray or white.

Carving Adventure Caricatures

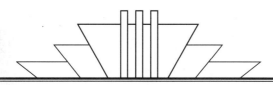

Previews

of Coming Attractions

THE BATTLE OF COLE CAMP

Starring Jonathan Rebel

Created on location at the Civil War battlefield near Cole Camp, Missouri, this figure is just a preview of the many patterns and carvings found in Maxwell's Woodcarving Shop in downtown Cole Camp.

JONATHAN REBEL is carved in the same manner as Pappy. Just follow the same step-by-step instructions used for carving the sailor. Many beard and mustache styles were popular during the Civil War. Watching old Civil War movies will help you create new and different styles when designing caricatures of your own. Uniform details are slightly different between the North and South. You may want to do additional research when carving authentic figures.

Serial Chapter #4

Rags the Wonder Dog in _Sticky Situations_

Last episode brought us to the edge of our seats as Rags fell from a logging truck and was about to be run over by a steam roller. In Chapter 4, Rags is saved in the nick of time by woodcarver Jim and finds companionship in the woodcarving shop. His dream of a home is nearly realized when a careless tourist drops Rags into a can of paint up to his eyes. Margie struggles desperately to save him from the sticky paint and restore his beautiful coat. Can Rags be saved? Will he go on to become a famed do-it-yourself project, or will he be sold as a sheep dog and taken to Australia? Don't miss Chapter 5: _Rags Eludes the Trash Man._

RAGS THE WONDER DOG is an excellent study in learning to carve hair. Sculpture the larger areas of curvy flowing hair, with a 6mm v-tool. Then use a 3mm v-tool for texturing. A few occasional deep cuts were made with the tip of a carving knife for depth and shadow.

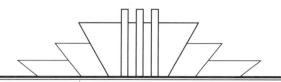

Selected Shorts

INDIAN ART FORMS

During the 1920s and 1930s, one of America's best-loved stars of the Silver Screen was the humorous Cherokee cowboy, Will Rogers. Will was proud of his Cherokee ancestry and often joked, "My ancestors may not have come over on the Mayflower, but they were here to meet the boat."

As a young man, I visited the Will Rogers Museum in Oklahoma and was quite impressed by the collection of beautiful Indian blankets displayed there. This visit really fueled my love and desire for fine Indian artwork and artifacts. After several years, I was able to acquire one of these beautiful hand-woven blankets for my home.

It is from my admiration and respect for this Indian art form that I have caricaturized these American Indians modeling their beautiful hand-woven blankets.

CHIEF RED BLANKET is designed to be very easy to carve. He has no visible arms or hands. The left heel is not really necessary, but some carvers may welcome the additional challenge. The eyes may be carved in a closed or open position, whichever you prefer.

The chief is modeling his colorful red blanket with a black and white border. He is wearing white feathers with dark brown tips. His moccasins are brown and have a small hole worn in the bottom.

BUFFALO SCOUT is wrapped in a light tan blanket with a yellow sun, highlighted with red-orange sun rays. The blanket is bordered with black and red trim. Be creative and try to design a color scheme of your own. The Indian blanket in my personal collection has a black background designed with many rainbow colors.

Carving Adventure Caricatures

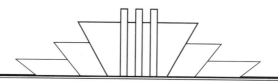

Feature Presentation
Part One

AMBUSH

Starring Broncho Buddy

One of the first and greatest adventure characters to ever appear on the Silver Screen was Broncho Billy (Max Anderson). As early as 1903, he began wearing a variety of flamboyant western costumes and creating character ideas that are still traditional today.

My version of this western hero will be called Broncho Buddy. In this feature he is wearing his U.S. Calvary costume. You may want to sharpen your tools before you saddle up with Broncho and ride off to Monument Valley in search of Indians.

Carving Adventure Caricatures

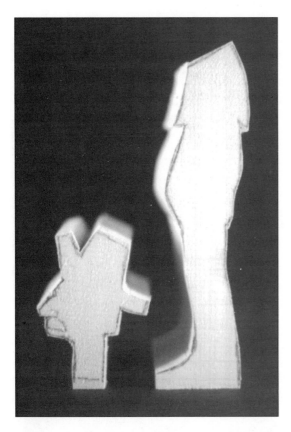

1 This 1950s version of a western hero was carved from two blocks of basswood. Use a block 6" x 2" x 2¹/₄" for his body and a block 3" x 2¹/₂" x 2¹/₂" for his head. First, trace the side view on the blocks and carefully bandsaw along the lines.

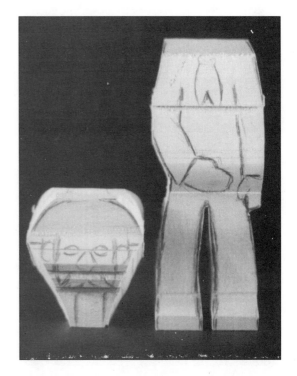

2 Now, lay the figure on its back and trace the front view. Carefully bandsaw along your new lines. Let's lay the head aside and begin carving the body.

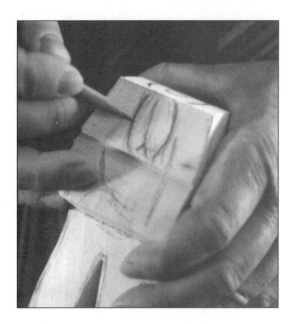

3 Using a pencil, boldly draw the outline of the neckerchief. The neckerchief appears on the front of the body, on the back of the body, and across the top of the shoulders.

4 Use a large v-tool to outline the neckerchief all around.

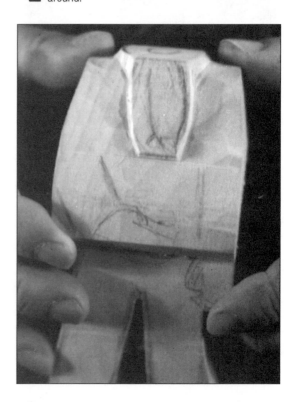

5 Use a knife to remove the wood from each side of the neckerchief on the front of the body. Then move to the top of the shoulders and the back, making the neckerchief stand out from the body.

6 This photo shows the neckerchief completely blocked out.

Carving Adventure Caricatures

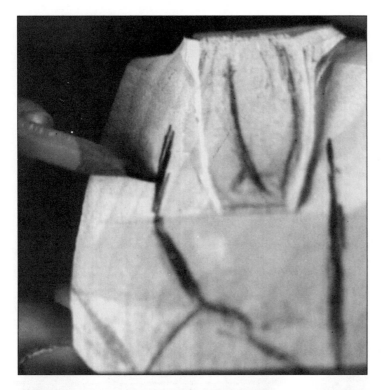

7 Next, use a pencil to draw the outline of the arms. Remember, it is important to use a pencil because stray marks can be erased. Ink from a pen or marker is permanent and will sink into the wood.

8 Using a woodcarving knife, carefully remove wood from in front of the left arm. The pencil marks will serve as your guide.

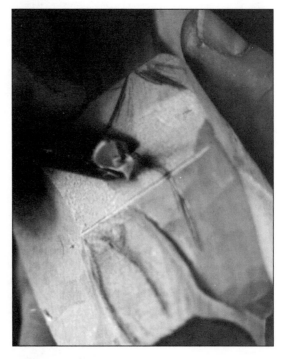

9 Outline the right hand and arm with a large v-tool.

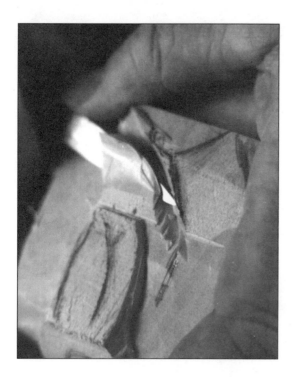

10 Flatten the chest area with your knife. Use small cuts to accomplish your goal. Two small cuts are just as good as one large one—and you're less likely to take off too much wood. Outline the stomach in the same manner.

11 After the chest and stomach are shaped, redraw the outline of the arms on the front, sides and back of the figure.

12 Using a woodcarving knife, remove wood from behind and under the right elbow.

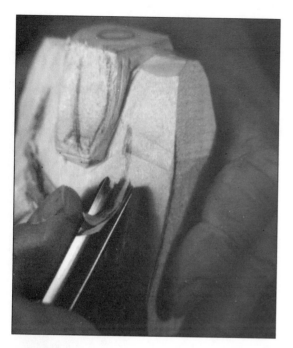

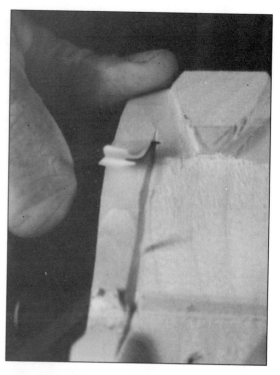

13 Next, separate the arms from the body with a large v-tool. Don't completely separate the arms and the body. A small indent is all you need to give definition to the arms.

14 Continue blocking in the arms until they reach the desired thickness.

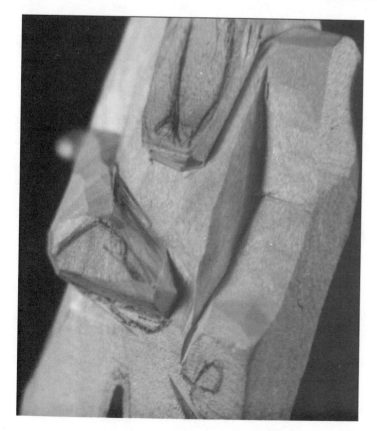

15 This photo shows a nicely blocked figure. Before you continue, check your carving to make sure that the arms are proportional and that each is the same thickness.

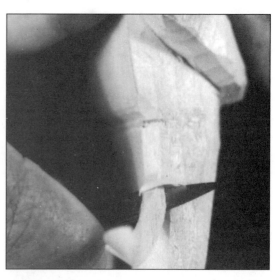

16 Now you're ready to begin shaping the legs. Because the legs were bandsawed from both sides, they need no additional blocking. Just use your woodcarving knife to begin rounding the front corner of the right leg.

17 Next, round the back corner of the right leg. Again, take small, exact cuts to avoid removing too much wood.

18 Next, round the inside corners of the legs and feet. When rounding and shaping the legs, keep in mind that calvary men lived for days in the saddle on nothing but beef jerky, water and soda biscuits. Their legs were usually thin and almost always bowed.

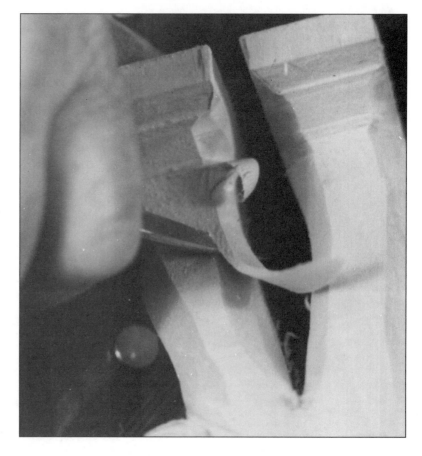

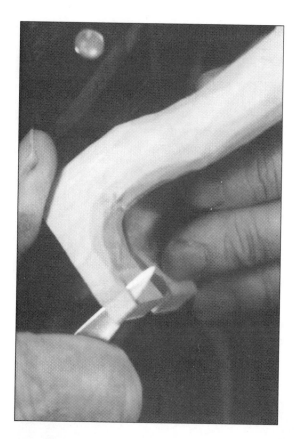

19 Before moving on to point the toes on Broncho Buddy's boots, check to make sure that both legs and both feet are equally proportioned. Trim away any excess wood.

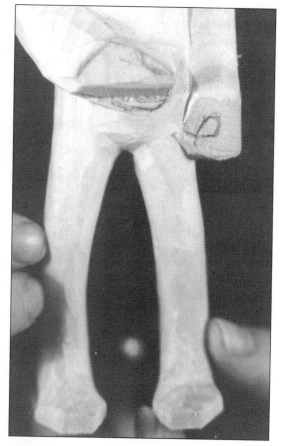

20 This photo shows nicely shaped feet and legs. Next, we'll move on to the arms. We'll add the details to his boots and pants later.

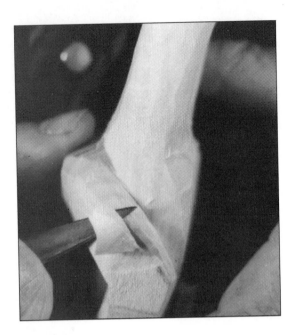

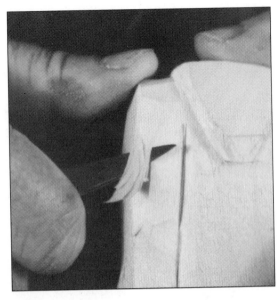

21 Begin rounding the arms by using a woodcarving knife to round the right arm and wrist area first.

22 Now, round and shape the left arm. Remember that calvary men were thin. If you give your figure thin legs, you'll have to give him thin arms as well.

23 Broncho Buddy's arms and wrists are nicely shaped. We're now ready to move on to his torso.

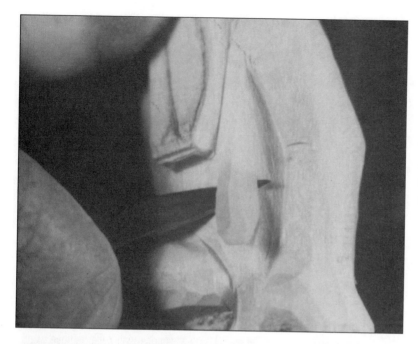

24 Use a woodcarving knife to begin shaping the rib cage and upper torso. Carvers with less experience may find this area easier to shape with an 8mm shallow gouge.

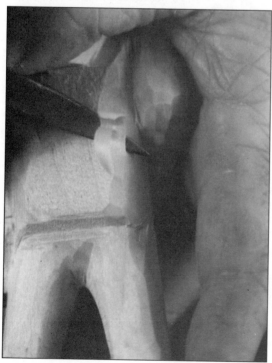

25 Round and shape the back and buttocks area with a knife. A thin torso will add to Broncho Buddy's character, so I'm going to take a little extra wood away from his waistline.

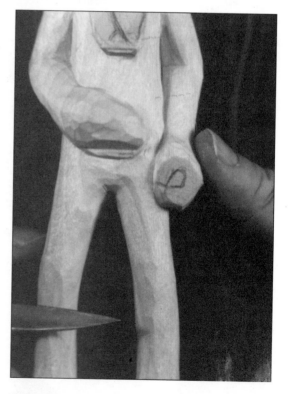

26 The body is now nicely shaped. Let's set the body aside now and begin working on the head.

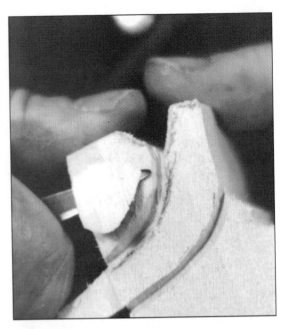

27 Begin work on Broncho Buddy's head by using a pencil to mark a dark outline around the edges of the hat brim. Cut along these marks with a large v-tool.

28 Using a woodcarving knife, remove wood from each side of the hat crown. Be careful to make both sides similar.

29 Once you get close to the hat brim, use a stop cut around the brim to make the chips from the crown come off cleanly. Continue to work on the crown until it reaches the desired thickness.

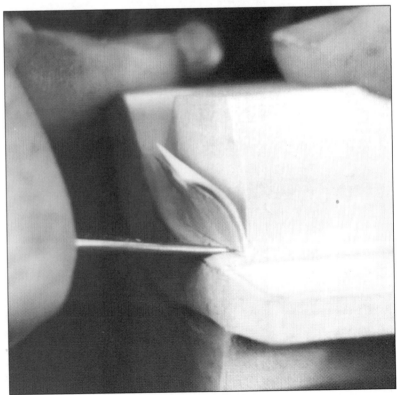

Carving Adventure Caricatures

30 Before you begin to remove wood from each side of the head, measure your pattern. Now draw on lines to show the width of the ears at the widest part.

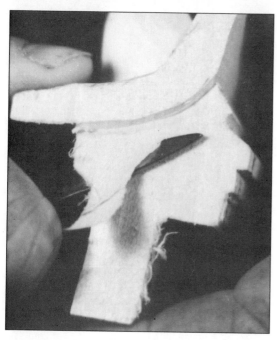

31 Using a woodcarving knife, remove the wood from each side of the head. You'll need to make stop cuts under the hat brim to make your chips

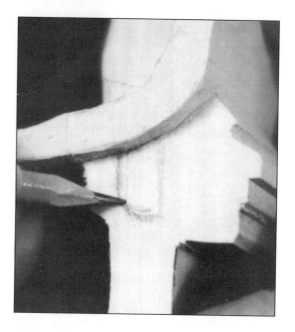

32 After carving away enough wood from each side of the head to reach the desired thickness at the ears, use a pencil to detail the area that will be used for the ears.

Feature Presentation, Part One

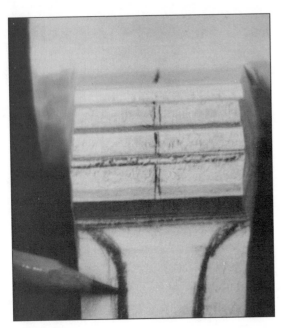

33 Using a pencil, redraw the front view of the neck. Add a centerline down the front of the nose.

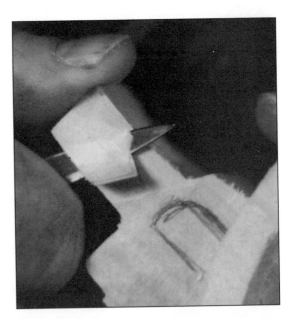

34 Cut the wood away from each side of the neck with a woodcarving knife.

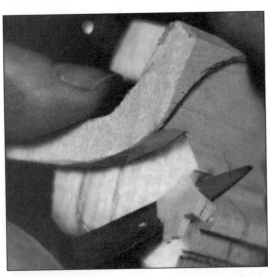

35 Draw on the front view of the turned up hat brim and begin to shape the front of the face. First thin each side of the nose, being careful not to actually point the nose. As you carve along the jaw area, you will probably remove a small amount of wood from the front part of the ears. Redraw any pencil marks you have removed from this area.

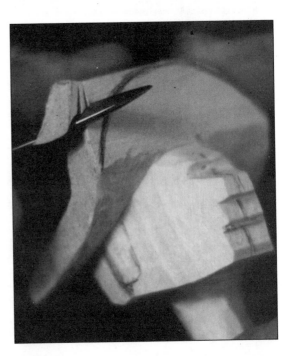

36 Round all four corners of the hat brim. Oops! I took off a little too much on one side. You may notice in the next photo where I glued a small piece on the side of the hat brim.

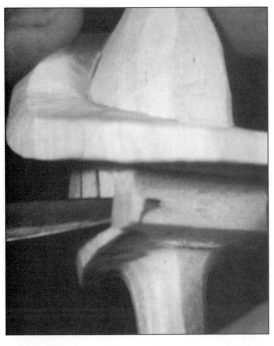

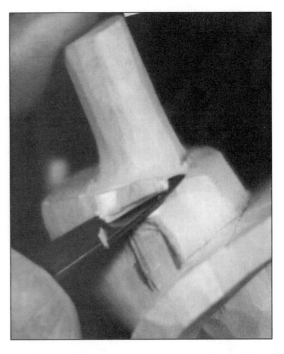

37 Use a woodcarving knife to round the corners on the back of the head just behind the ears.

38 Still using the knife, remove the wood directly below the ear to help shape the upper neck.

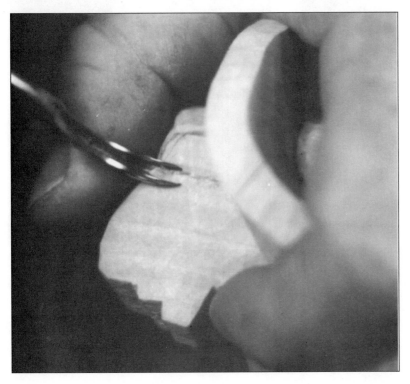

39 Use a small v-tool to block out the front and back of the ears.

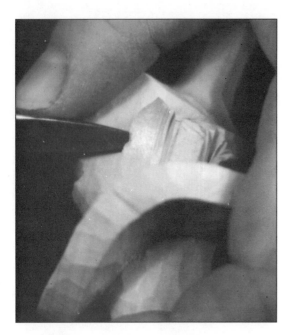

40 Use a woodcarving knife to remove a little more wood from the sideburns and the area immediately behind the ears.

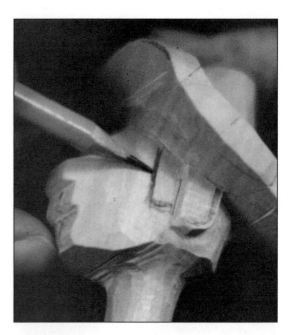

41 Now, draw on the sideburns.

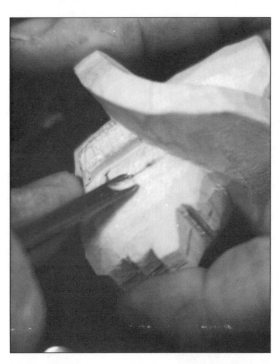

42 Block out the sideburns using a small v-tool.

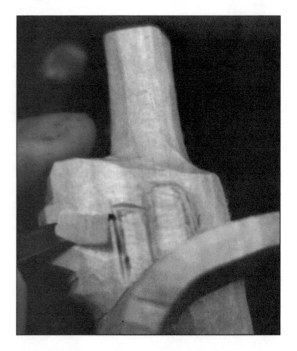

43 Clean up the area around the sideburns a little more by using your knife to remove wood from the sides of the face and from below the sideburns.

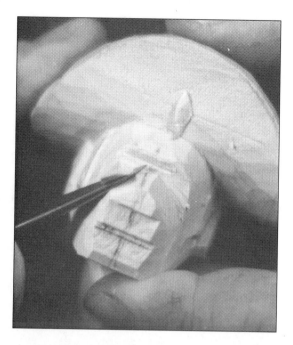

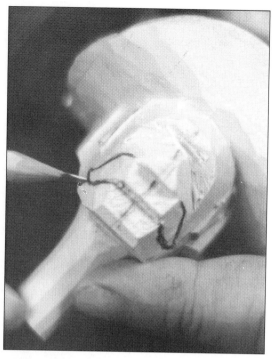

44 Angle the top of the nose toward the centerline that you drew earlier. This photo shows the left side completed. I'm now cutting the right side.

45 Draw on Broncho Buddy's mustache.

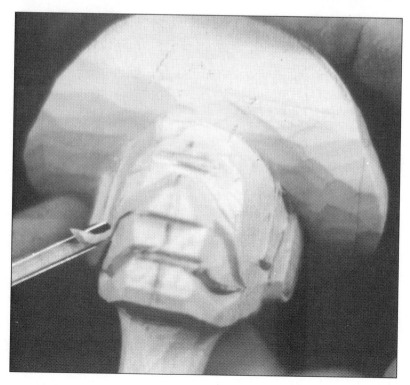

46 Use a large v-tool to block out the mustache. Once again, this photo shows the left side completed. I'm working on the right side.

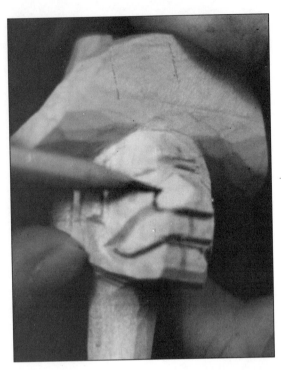

47 Check your pattern for placement and draw the nostrils on the face with a pencil.

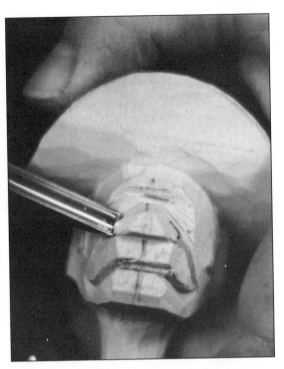

48 Use a 5mm gouge to make a stop cut around the nostril.

49 Use the same 5mm gouge to remove a small amount of wood behind the nostril and across the top of the mustache. You'll note that the left side is completed, and I'm working on the right side.

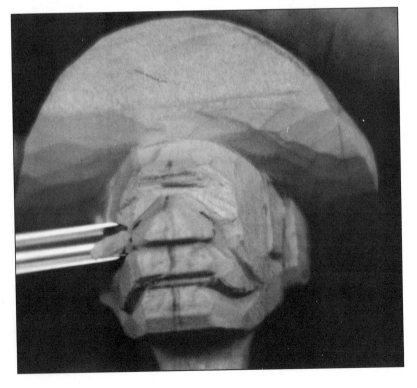

Carving Adventure Caricatures

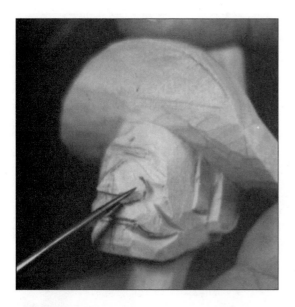

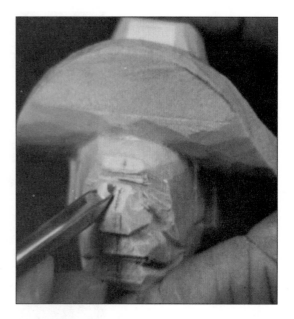

50 Broncho Buddy's nose is completely blocked out at this point, but it still needs some more shaping. Using a woodcarving knife, remove a little bit of wood from under the nostrils at the widest part of the nose. This will make the nostrils appear higher at their widest part.

51 Now, remove a small portion of wood along each side of the bridge of the nose with a 5mm gouge. This cut will create the upper shape of the nostril. I've finished the left side and am now working on the right side.

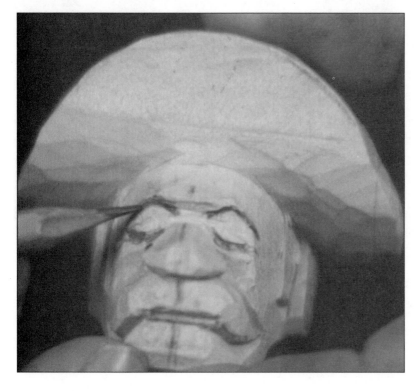

52 Now, let's work on the eyes. Begin by drawing on the eyebrows and the lower eye contour lines.

53 Shape the contour of the eye with a 4mm gouge. Carve along the eyebrow line, keeping the tool just inside the line.

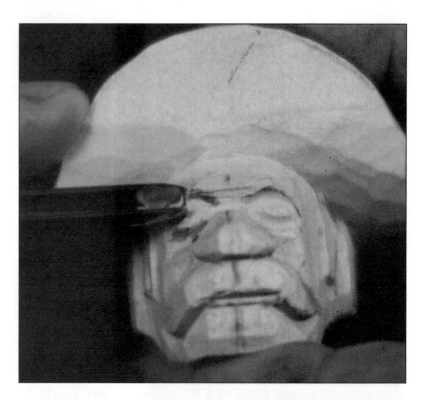

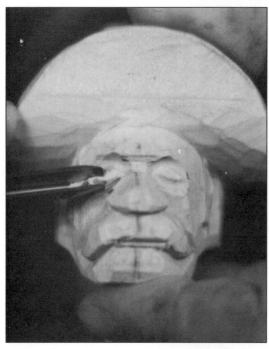

54 Repeat the same process along the bottom contour lines of the eye.

55 Now that the face is nicely blocked, take a knife and smooth up the face just a little to prepare the figure for more serious detail. Carve off the centerline and clean the saw marks from the top of his nose. Check around the nostrils for roughness and smooth the chin area around the mustache.

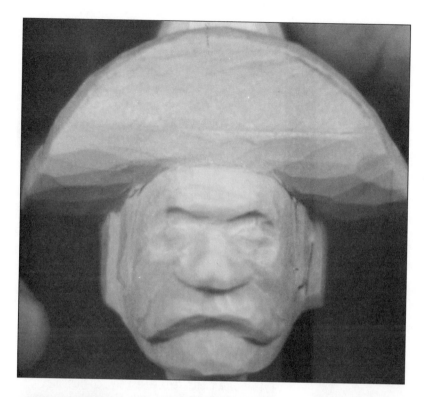

56 Broncho Buddy's face is now smoothed and ready for more detail.

57 Now, let's open Broncho Buddy's eyes so he can spot any Indians hiding in the brush. Begin by drawing on the upper and lower eyelids.

58 Using a small v-tool, follow these lines as closely as possible to cut the actual eyes. The left eye is completed, and I am now cutting the right eye.

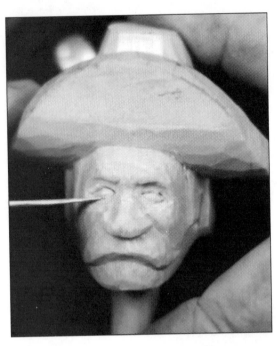

59 To make these eye cuts a little deeper and as crisp as possible, clean the cuts with a very small, sharply pointed knife.

60 Using a knife, remove the wood from the surface of the eyeball. This is the area between the upper and lower eyelids. To make the eyeball look round, remove more wood from the corners of the eye.

61 With a very sharp pencil, draw in the iris. By placing the iris in the corners of the eye, you can make it appear that Broncho is looking to the left or right.

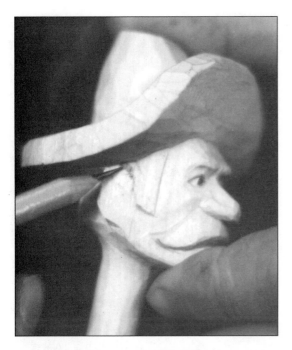

62 Check your pattern and draw on the top curvature of the ear with a pencil.

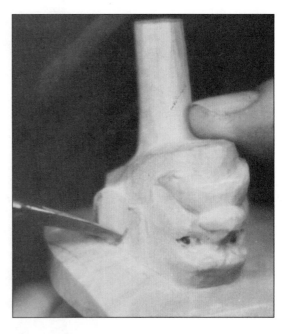

63 Use a small knife and make a stop cut around the top of the ears.

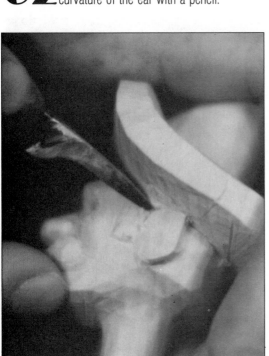

64 Now trim the sideburns away from the top of the ears.

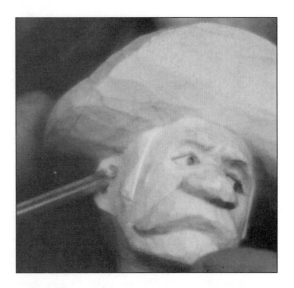

65 To add detail to the inside of the ears, first draw a small "s" inside the ear. Remove the wood from behind the letter with a very small gouge. This will give the appearance of a slightly detailed ear. Beginning carvers can get the same effect just by scooping out a small rounded cavity.

66 To begin shaping the lower lip, use a 4mm gouge. Remove the wood between the lower lip and the chin.

67 Carving hair is actually quite simple, but can be a stumbling block for many carvers. First, draw locks of hair on the mustache.

68 Next, take a small v-tool and cut directly on your pencil lines, breaking the larger body of hair into smaller sections. These cuts are fairly bold.

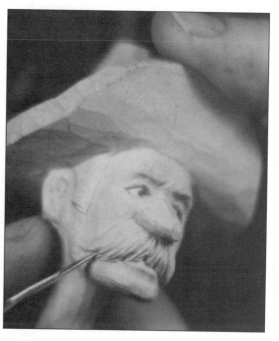

69 Now take the same small v-tool and texture each lock with very fine lines.

70 Using a very small knife, separate the outer most tips of each lock of hair. Don't try to put a painted tip on each follicle.

71 To detail the sideburns, draw three large locks of hair on each side. These locks should slant down and back toward the ear.

72 Using a small v-tool, cut directly on these lines to shape the sideburns into locks of hair.

73 Use the same small v-tool to carve very fine lines on these locks of hair. Once again, use a very fine pointed knife to separate the ends of the locks.

74 Now that the sideburns and mustache are completed, let's carve Broncho Buddy's eyebrows. Eyebrows are a very important part of a caricature's expression and should be applied with care. For this figure we will use a fine-textured hair technique. Rougher hair is often used on the crustier caricatures, but Broncho is a hero and must be handsome.

Using the smallest v-tool, carve very fine lines slanting upward and outward across the eyebrow. Holding the figure upside down may make carving easier—just be sure that you are carving in the correct direction.

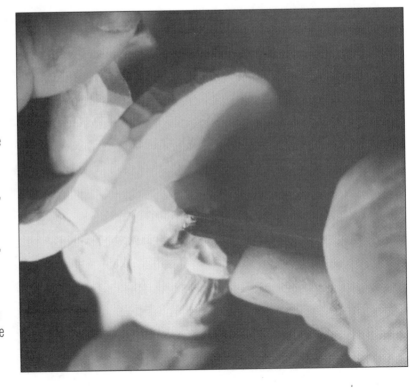

Carving Adventure Caricatures

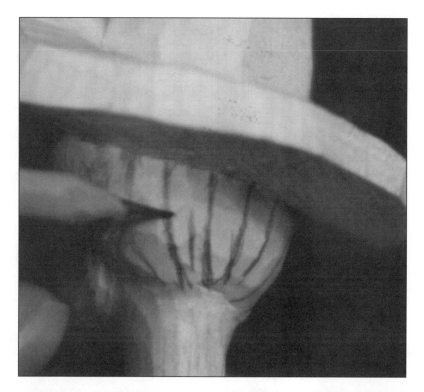

75 To carve the hair on the back of the head, follow the same procedures. First, use a pencil to draw sections on the hair. For the best-looking results, draw these locks angling down and toward the center of the neck.

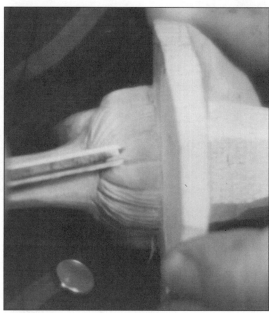

76 Use a small v-tool to separate the locks of hair. Try not to make each lock the same size. The hair will look more natural if you have some large locks and some small ones.

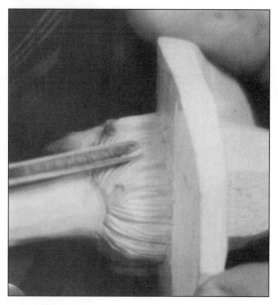

77 Finally, texture the hair on the back of the head with the same small v-tool. After the fine details have been carved on the back of the head, you may again wish to take a small knife and separate the locks at the ends.

78 Now that Broncho's hair and face are complete, let's finish carving the hat. Finish thinning the hat brim first. Add a few wrinkle cuts to the thinned brim to make the hat look less stiff.

79 Finish rounding and shaping the crown of the hat.

80 Most calvary men creased their hats lengthwise along the crown. Use a 5mm deep gouge to add the crease.

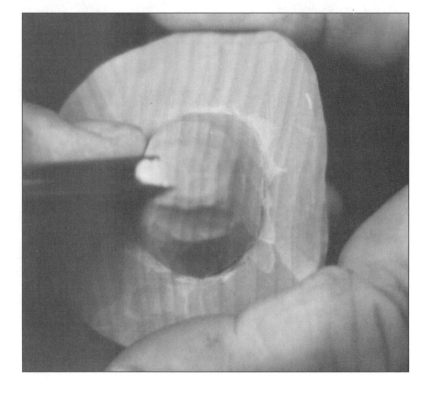

81 Using a sharp pencil draw on the hat band, Check your pattern for reference.

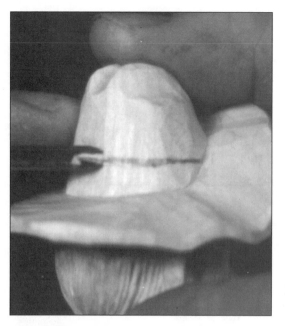

82 With a small v-tool, carve around the hat band.

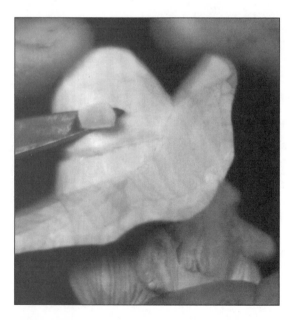

83 After outlining the hat band, remove a little more wood from the sides of the hat crown. This makes the hat band appear to stand out just a little.

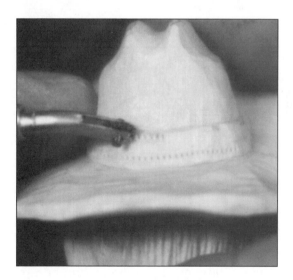

84 Stitching hat bands, vests and other pieces of clothing can make a western caricature look even more authentic. Use a punch or an artist's pounce wheel to add detail to Broncho's hat band.

Now, let's take a break to sharpen our tools. We'll continue carving Broncho after the Intermission.

Intermission

One
Dip
or
Two

A good adventure movie is never complete without a bag of popcorn or a candy treat. Let's stretch our legs and sharpen our tools, and take time out for a dip or two before we return to finish Broncho Buddy.

Intermission

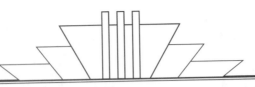

Feature Presentation
Part 2

AMBUSH

Starring Broncho Buddy

Now that we've had time to grab a bite to eat, stretch our limbs and sharpen our tools, let's return to carving Broncho Buddy.

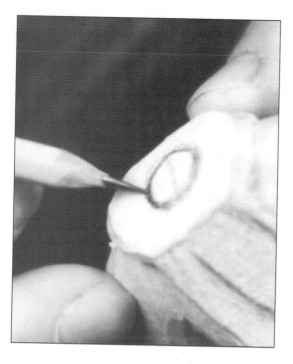

85 Draw a hole in the body to receive Broncho's neck. Make sure the hole is centered on the shoulders.

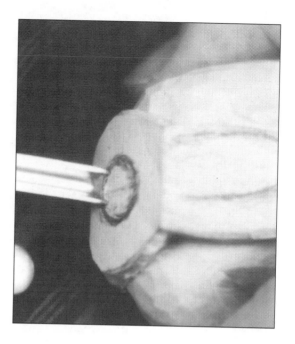

86 Take a 5mm deep gouge and make a stop cut on the neckline, pushing the gouge directly into the top of the neckerchief.

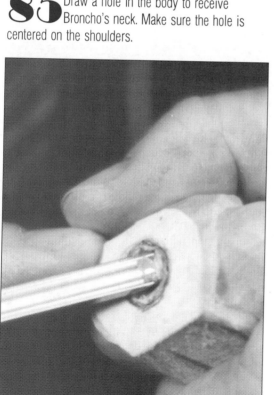

87 Using the 5mm deep gouge, begin removing wood from the neck hole. It is important to always keep making stop cuts before using the gouge to remove wood. The stop cuts will make your chips come off clean and prevent you from removing too much wood. As the hole gets deeper, be careful not to pry or overload your gouge. This is a perfect place to break a gouge.

Some carvers drill their neck holes, but if the drill slips, you will be throwing away hours of work.

Feature Presentation, Part Two

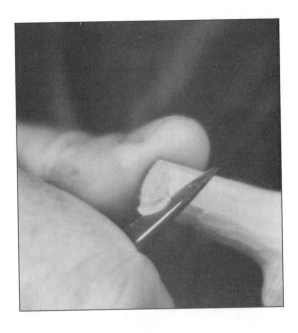

88 This photo shows a good fit for the neck.

89 Once you have a good fit, begin shortening the neck a small amount at a time until the neck appears to be the proper length.

90 This photo shows the neck carved to the right length and fitted into the body. Do not glue yet. You may need to trim it a tiny bit more after the neckerchief is finished.

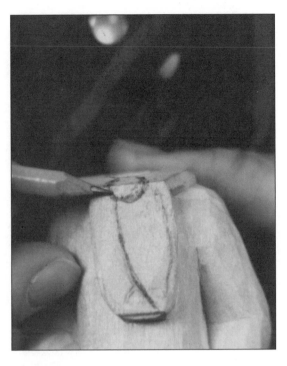

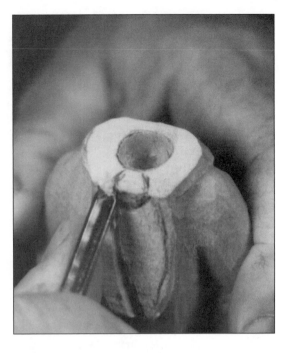

91 Finish the neckerchief by first drawing on a large knot.

92 Use a v-tool to outline the knot and to separate the front part of the scarf into two sections.

93 Remove a small amount of wood from the front and top of the neckerchief until the knot stands out just a little.

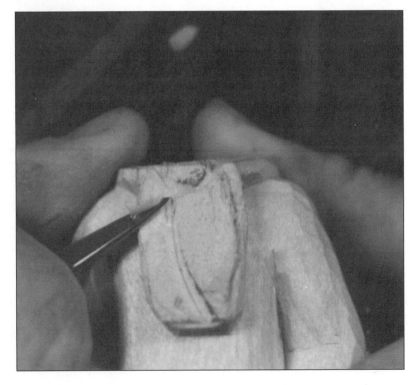

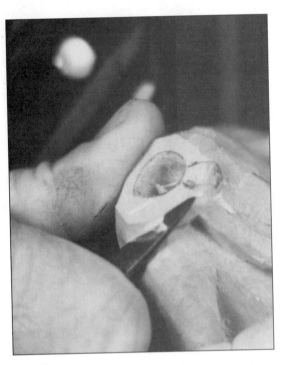

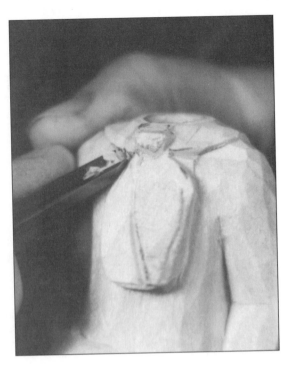

94 Shape the top edges of the neckerchief.

95 Use a v-tool or tip of a woodcarving knife to trim around the knot.

96 Use the tip of a knife to make a notch separating the neckerchief corners.

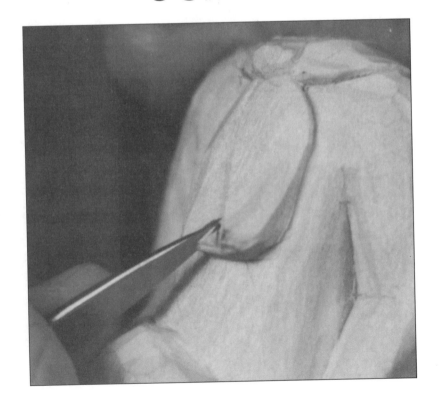

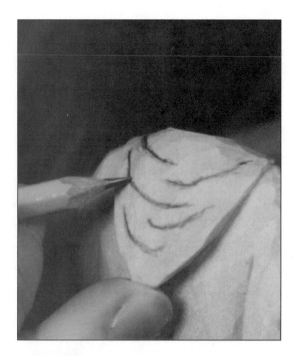

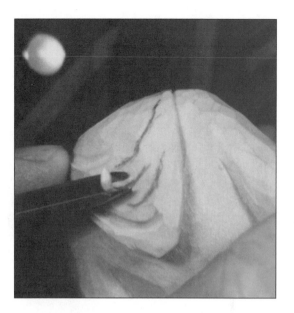

97 With a pencil, draw wrinkles on the neckerchief, both front and back. Try to make them look quite random.

98 Carve along these lines with a gouge. I use more than one size gouge so that I have more than one size wrinkle in both front and back. Smooth the gouge marks slightly with the tip of a knife.

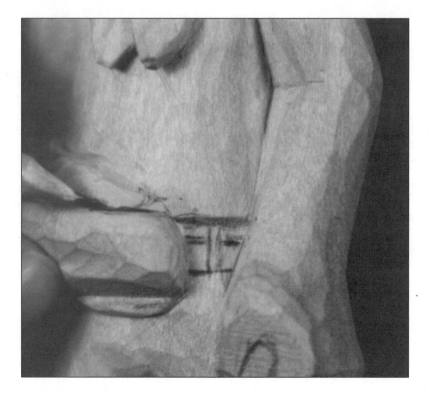

99 Draw on the belt and the pant line on the front and back of the figure. The line for the belt will also separate the thumb and fingers on the right hand. Later, the thumb will be hooked under the belt.

100 Study the pattern carefully. Then, use a small v-tool to outline the pants, belt and belt loops, in both front and back.

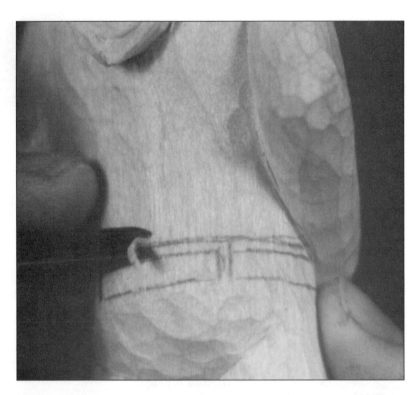

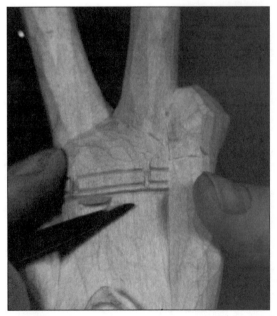

101 After outlining the top of the pants, use your knife to remove wood from the shirt so it appears that the shirt is tucked inside the pants, both front and back.

102 Trim a little wood off the pants around the belt and belt loops with a woodcarving knife. This will make the belt stand out from the rest of the body.

103 Begin to finish the hand by first drawing on the cuff.

104 Use a woodcarving knife to make a stop cut around the cuff.

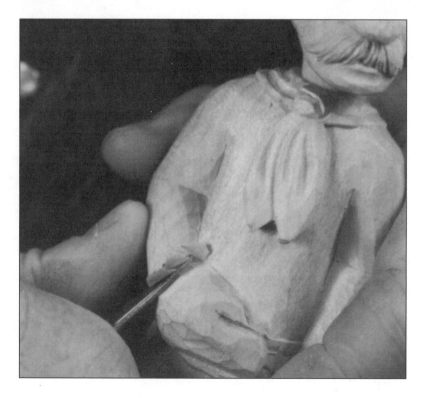

105 Now, cut toward the stop cut, removing wood slowly and cleanly from the wrist.

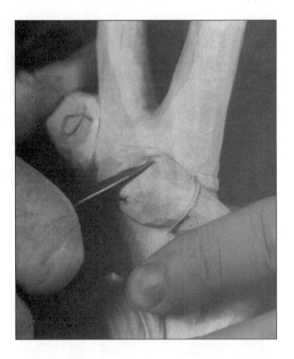

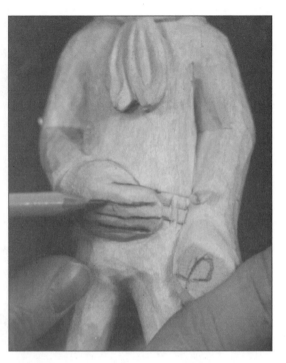

106 Shape the back of the fingers with a woodcarving knife. Study your pattern closely for reference.

107 Use a pencil to draw on the fingers.

**108** Using a v-tool, follow along the pencil marks to outline the fingers.

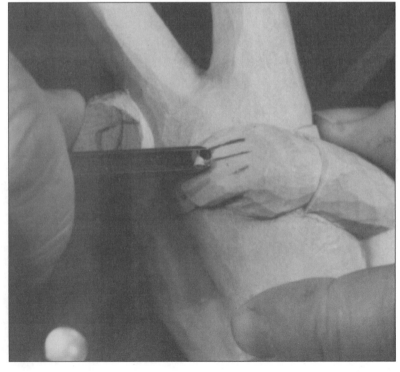

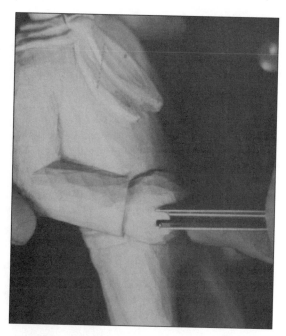

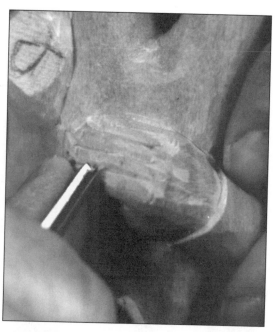

109 Carve between the knuckles and up the back of the hand using a 4mm deep gouge. These cuts will add more detail to the back of the hand.

110 Detail the fingernails and knuckles with a small v-tool. This step is optional, though I usually take the time to add these little details on a carving this size.

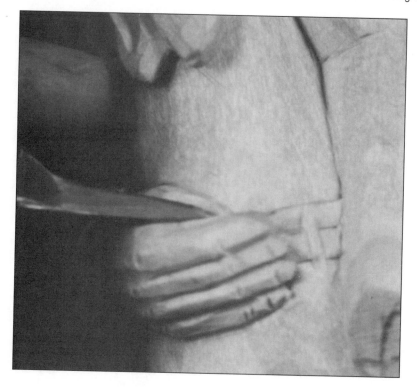

111 With a very small knife, remove the wood from the front of the thumb so that the thumb appears to be hooked behind the belt.

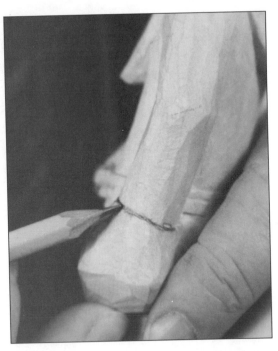

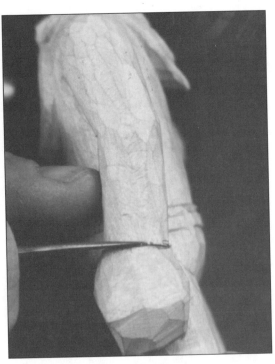

112 To carve the left hand, begin by drawing the outline of the shirt cuff onto the wood.

113 Next, take your knife and make a stop cut around this line.

114 Now, take your knife and remove wood from the wrist.

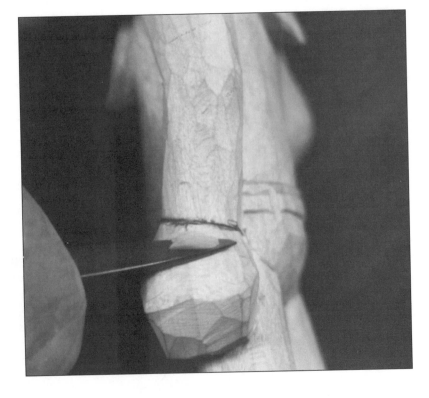

Carving Adventure Caricatures

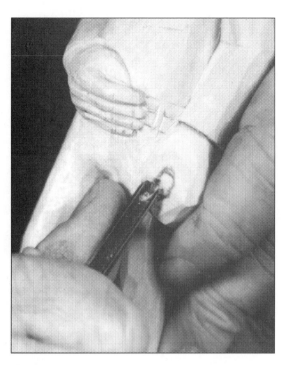

115 Use a v-tool to outline the thumb.

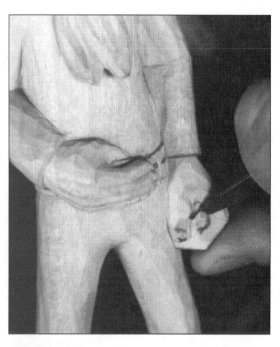

116 Remove enough wood from the front of the hand to make the thumb appear to stand out just a little.

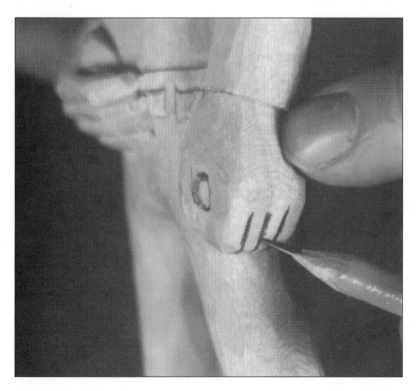

117 Draw an outline of the fingers on the left hand. Also redraw the hole for his rifle. (This mark was removed when shaping the front part of his hand.)

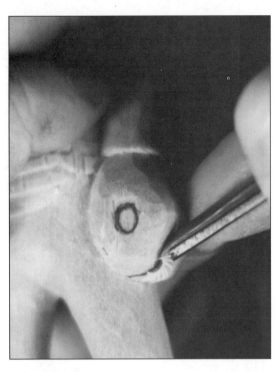

118 Use a v-tool to outline the fingers on the left hand.

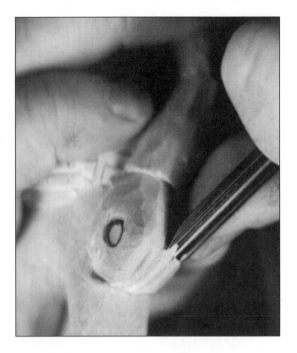

119 Shape the back of the knuckles and the back of the left hand with a 4mm deep gouge.

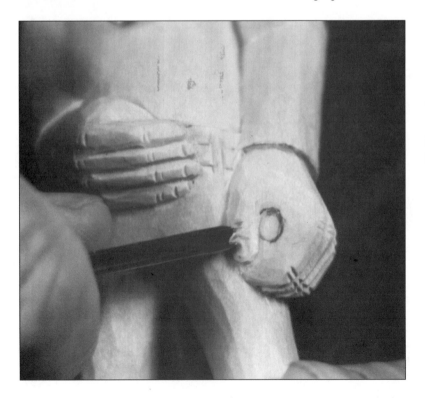

120 Using a small v-tool, add detail to the knuckles and outline the left thumbnail.

121 To make the hole in Broncho's hand f[...] the rifle, use a 2mm deep gouge.

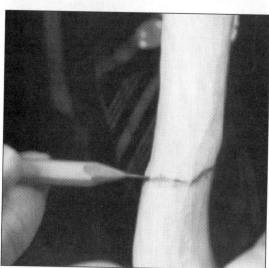

122 With a pencil, draw the outline of the top of Broncho's boots. A calvary man's boots are slightly different from a cowboy's boots. Study the pattern closely.

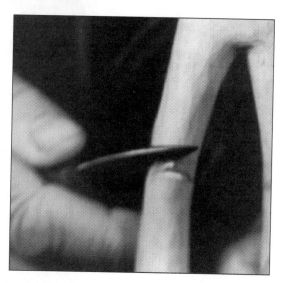

123 Using a small v-tool or woodcarving knife, outline the top of the boots. Trim away a little of the pant legs so Broncho's pants just brush the top of his boots.

Feature Presentation, Part Two

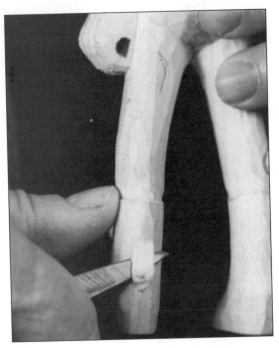

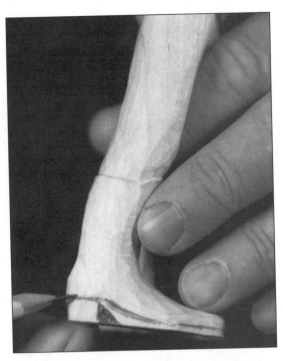

124 Shape the boot heels by removing a little wood just above the heel. The right leg is finished. I am now carving the left leg.

125 Using a pencil, draw the outline of the heels and the soles of the boots.

126 Now use your knife to make a notch between the heels and the soles.

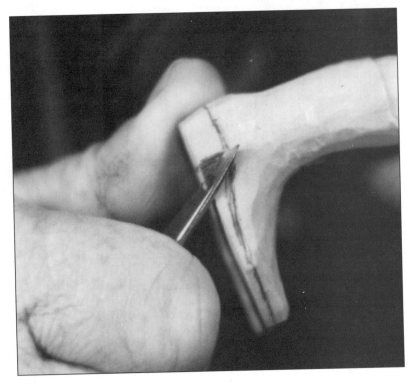

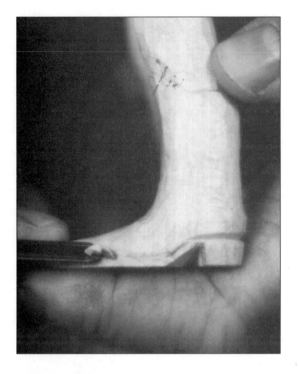

127 Use a small v-tool to outline the soles of Broncho's boots.

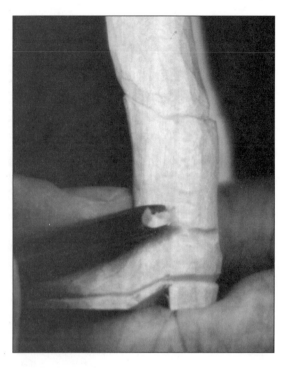

128 Make wrinkles across the ankles with a 4mm deep gouge.

129 Use a 2mm deep gouge to put a few wrinkles across the top of the toes.

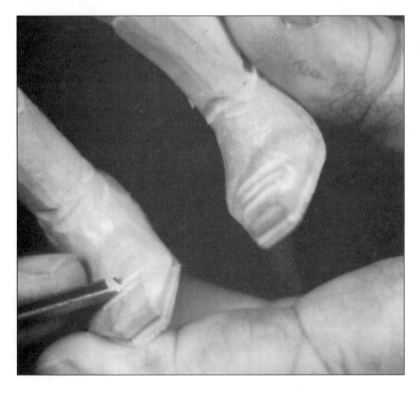

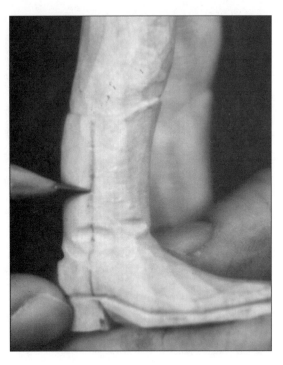

130 Using a pencil, draw a seam on the sides of the boots.

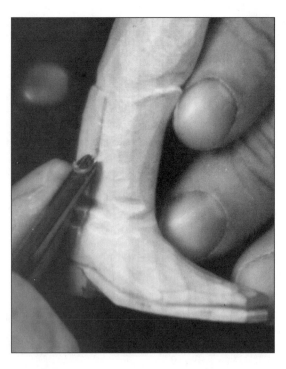

131 Use a small v-tool to carve the seam.

132 With a small pounce wheel or punch, make stitches along the seam.

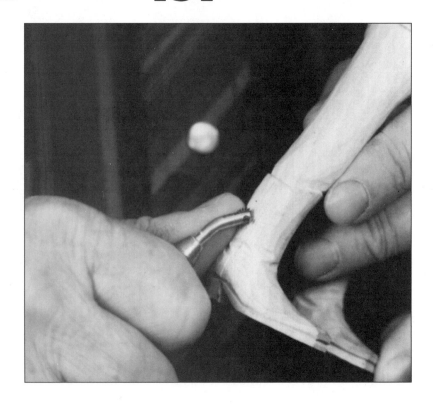

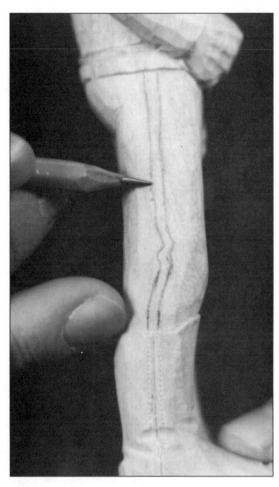

133 Using a pencil, draw the outline of the stripes on Broncho's pants.

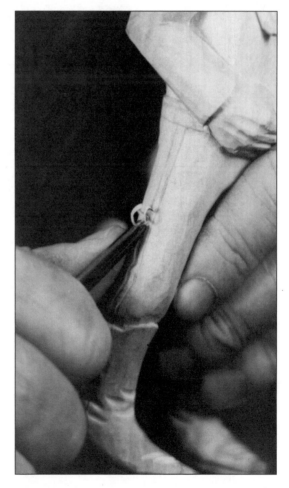

134 Carve the stripes with a small v-tool.

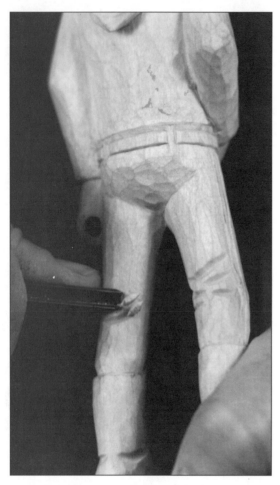

135 With a large v-tool, carve the wrinkles behind the knees.

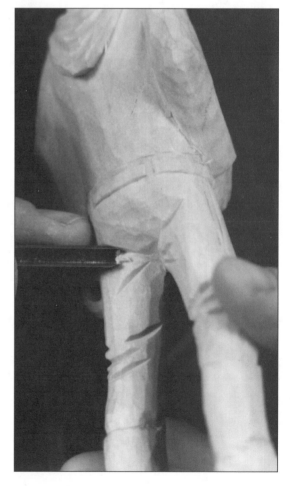

136 Using the same large v-tool, carve the wrinkles under the buttocks.

137 Still using the large v-tool, mark wrinkles in the front bend of the arms. Also make smaller wrinkles where the arms attach to the shoulders.

138 Use a 4mm deep gouge to make a few wrinkles in the back of the shirt.

Feature Presentation, Part Two

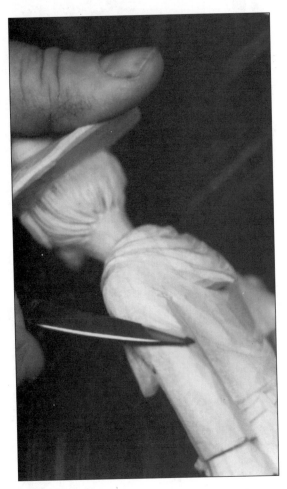

139 Add a few folds or wrinkles on the backs of the arms, starting at the elbow and running upward. Use a knife for these cuts. You'll also want to make a few wrinkles running down the back of the arms.

140 Give Broncho a bit of military rank by adding a chevron to each sleeve with a small v-tool.

Carving Adventure Caricatures

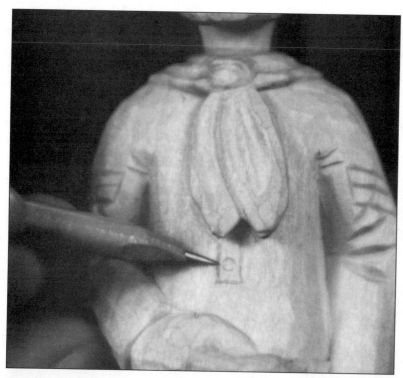

141 Draw the outline of the opening on the front of Broncho's shirt. Also draw in a button.

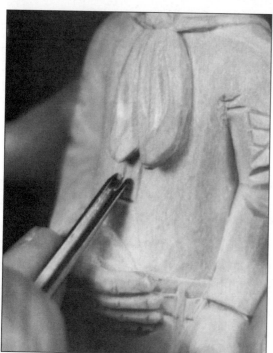

142 Use a small v-tool to carve the opening on the front of his shirt.

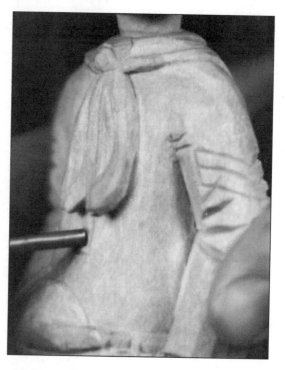

143 Use a button punch to make the button.

Feature Presentation, Part Two

Broncho's hat is a mixture of white, Mars black and raw umber. His scarf is cadmium yellow mixed with a small amount of white. For the a chevron on his sleeve use yellow oxide. Thin these colors only slightly.

Broncho's shirt is Marge's version of royal blue—cobalt blue mixed with Mars black. Use the same color for his pants, but add a small amount of white to make them lighter than the shirt. Color his belt and boots with Mars black.

To paint the gun metal, use Mars black. Burnt umber is used to paint the stock.

144 Carve Broncho a rifle and insert it into his hand.

Painting Tips—Broncho's Face

Begin by painting the whites of Broncho's eyes. Use a flesh color on his face and hands. I use Folk Art Acrylic skin tone, thinned only slightly with water. To highlight the cheeks, mix a small amount of cadmium red medium with the flesh color. Apply this mix to the cheek area while the paint on his face is still damp. Blend the two colors with a clean brush. Use the same procedure for Broncho's fingernails and his knuckles. You can also highlight the inside of the ear. Use thinned Mars black for the hair and a stronger Mars black for the eyebrows.

When your carving is dry, apply an antiquing finish of burnt umber oil and boiled linseed oil. Wipe the carving dry and your carving is complete.

145 Finally, glue Broncho's head into his neck. Position the head so the figure appears to be relaxed. Be sure that the eyes are looking in the same direction.

The Late Show

Adventure Island

**Starring
Willie
Survive**

Marooned on a tiny island with nothing but his trusting carving knife, Willie offers plenty of challenge for carvers who like to put a little action into their figure.

Willie has carved a notch into a piece of driftwood for each marooned day. Although his note in the bottle has drifted back to shore, his joyous expression suggests that today there may be a ship on the horizon.

Carve the palm branches separately and insert them into the holes drilled in the trunk. Carve the driftwood, knife, dead fish and bottle separately and attach them with tiny dowels. Use a small dowel when attaching the palm tree to the base.

Top View

Palm branches - Make four or five.

Side View

Drill Holes

Side Views

Front View

This pattern should be worked from front view for best results.

Dowel

SEND HELP

Carving Adventure Caricatures

Top Ten
Favorite Movies

 Kills More Bear

 Armed and Dangerous

 Missing Sapphire

 Missing Clue

 The Big Story

 The Turbulent Clouds

 The Front Line

 Blockade Runner

 The Villain Strikes Again

 Eagle Eye McDanger

Kills More Bear

Watching adventure films featuring American Indians is a good way to be entertained and do research at the same time.

Many western movies star real Indians. Two of my old favorites are Jay Silverheels and Iron Eyes Cody. Their buckskin costumes and eagle feathers are typical of what many Indians wore in early westerns. Watching these great Indian actors always inspires me to try and create a new Indian caricature of my own.

KILLS MORE BEAR is the most respected hunter in his tribe. He stands proudly on his freshly skinned bear rug. Only moderate skills are required to carve this mighty hunter. A little roughness will only enhance his overall appearance.

When carving this project, follow the general procedures in Movie Time News. Try texturing his knife blade with a 4mm gouge. The effect will be that of chipped stone. Texturing the base will require some time. The hair on the rug can be applied with your smallest v-tool. (Ribbon-winning wildlife carvers often use a woodburning tool for very fine hair and fur detail.) His headband and belt are a colorful polka dot cloth. He wears a bear-claw necklace, a trophy of his last big hunt.

Armed and Dangerous
Starring Murphy Blowgart

 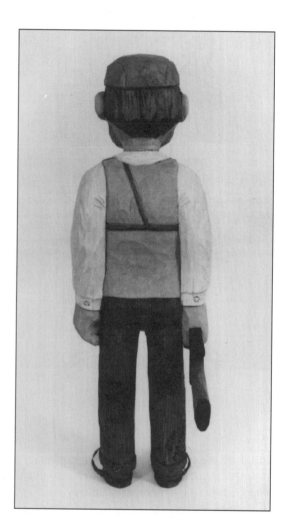

Anyone who watches old movies is sure to have seen a few of the gangster films. Hollywood gave these tough guys lots of character. Gangster patterns make great projects, and the rougher you make them the more original they appear.

MURPHY's unshaven face is textured with a 3 mm v-tool. The two-piece machine gun and cigar are carved and inserted separately.

The iris of the eye is painted off-center and looking to the right to relax the appearance of the figure. Most depression era business suits were dark in color with small pinstripes. Wing-tip shoes were very popular at this time.

Top Ten Favorite Movies

The Missing Sapphires
Starring Gary (Butch) Gant

"Who Done It?" No mystery movie is complete without the presence of a slippery cat burglar. I have named my burglar Butch. He is wearing old style sneakers and carries a flashlight and pry bar.

BUTCH is an easy figure to carve, however, you may find carving the eyes behind the mask a bit of a challenge. The sweater is textured with a very small gouge. Use a small gouge to create the appearance of elastic on the turtle neck, wrist and waistband of the sweater. His clothing should be painted in all dark colors, best for lurking about in the shadows.

The Missing Clue
Starring Mike Malone

Super sleuth and solver of all crimes, Malone is embarked upon his endless pursuit of catching the cat burglar. Sneaking about in his trench coat and wing-tip shoes, he never misses a clue.

MIKE MALONE requires intermediate carving skill. Malone's hat is brown. His trench coat is tan and is badly wrinkled by the cold, damp night air.

Top Ten Favorite Movies

The Big Story
Starring Jane Drew

Jane Drew, a top reporter for a large metropolitan newspaper, is ready for a busy day of on the spot news investigation and coverage. Even though her relentless curiosity is always getting her into trouble, she still manages to look great wearing the latest fashions.

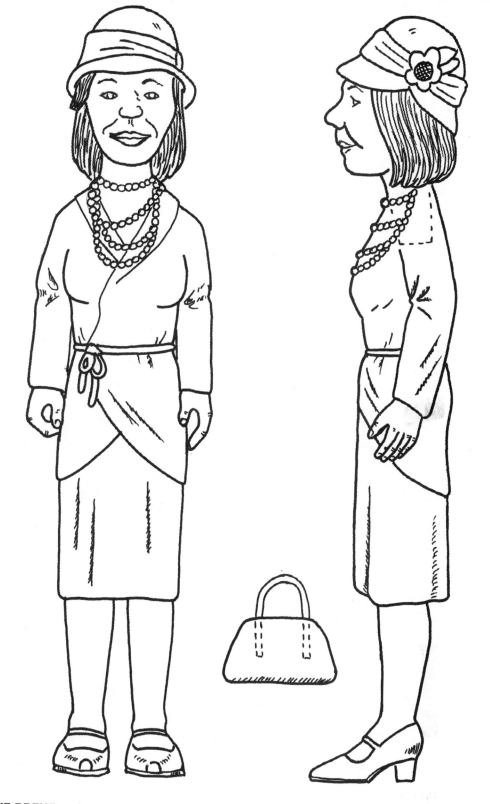

JANE DREW's head is carved separately and turned to the left to make her look more at ease. Her purse is also carved separately and is attached with a piece of wire. Jane likes light colored dresses and pretty hats to match. The tiny print pattern on her dress was applied with the point of a toothpick.

Top Ten Favorite Movies

The Turbulent Clouds
Starring Ace Anderson

Created in the 1930s, one of Hollywood's favorite adventure characters, was the barnstorming pioneer aviator. He flies his primitive air-ship to all points of the globe looking for excitement and fortune.

Carving Adventure Caricatures

Dressed in typical clothing of their era, my aviators often hold bent or broken props that are installed separately). Fur-textured collars can be achieved with a 2mm gouge. The reflection on the goggles is a light gray color on the lens that is then shaded with white.

Top Ten Favorite Movies

The Front Line
Starring Sergeant Steele

In the film, *Battleground,* James Whitmore portrayed a tough tobacco-chewing sergeant who strapped his feet in blankets to protect them from the bitter cold. Sergeant Steele is my caricature of a war hero.

SERGEANT STEELE, his rifle bayonet stuck in the snow, warms his hands over a flaming oil barrel. I have also wrapped his feet in blankets for additional comfort. The helmet straps and cigar are added separately.

When painting the base, the snow should appear to be melted close to the barrel. Add a few foot prints and jeep tracks in the snow for additional realism.

Top Ten Favorite Movies

The Blockade Runner
Starring Distributor Dan

The roar of speeding engines and the sound of squealing tires has been filling theater auditoriums, since man first began driving cars. My favorite car chase scenes are in the movie, *Thunder Road.* In this action-packed adventure film, the star, a Tennessee mountain boy, souped up his old car and was running moonshine liquor throughout Harlem County, Tennessee. Watching him crash through blockades and outrun revenuers with old Fords for years gave me inspiration for this caricature I call Distributor Dan.

DISTRIBUTOR DAN requires only moderate carving skills, however, a few nice effects can be accomplished by carving hair on his chest. He carries a two-piece wrench in one hand and a distributor and shaft in the other. Small black thread is inserted into the spark plug wire recepticle for realism.

Paint lots of dirt and grease on Dan's coveralls. And add your favorite oil company's logo patch over the upper pocket.

The Villain Strikes Again

Villains were first seen in theater plays and later on movie screens. Hollywood has created a large selection of these scoundrels for us to love or hate. Either way they make great woodcarving projects. The ones I like to carve are the cloak-and-dagger types.

These vile, unscrupulous rascals would often tie lonely maidens to sawmills and railroad tracks until the young women would promise marriage or give up the title to their land. In this scene the villain has tied Pretty Polly to a railroad crossing sign and has stolen her property deed.

THE VILLAIN is a very easy project. He has cold, evil eyes and a thin, curly mustache. The dagger and deed are carved separately.

Top Ten Favorite Movies

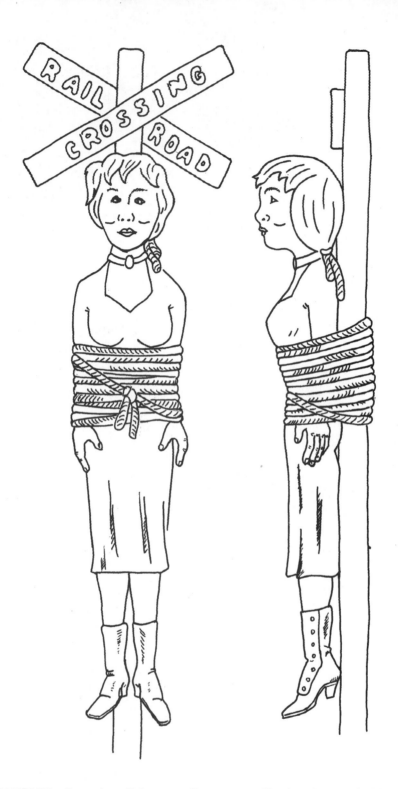

PRETTY POLLY will require a little more effort to carve. Her face is carved with very small facets to achieve a feminine look. The eyes are large and excited and looking away from the villain. Her hands are struggling to get free. The railroad crossing sign was carved separately and glued to the post. It is very effective to carve or paint a bit of railroad track on the base.

Carving Adventure Caricatures

Lost Treasure in the Jungle

Starring Eagle Eye McDanger

In recent years, Hollywood has been remaking the old 1930s cliff-hanger serials into block-buster features. For fifteen minutes each week, serials such as *Lost City In the Jungle,* would build to an exciting event, only to be continued next week in another chapter. In the end, the hero was always triumphant finding the lost treasure and winning the beautiful girl. My imaginary hero is called *Eagle Eye McDanger.*

Top Ten Favorite Movies

Carving Adventure Caricatures

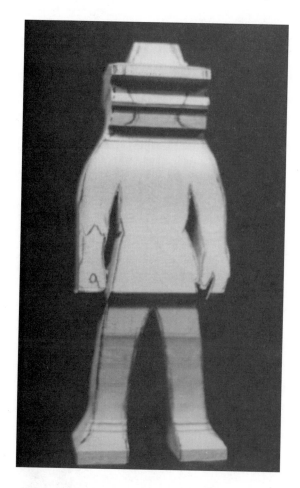

1 Begin with a block of wood large enough to accommodate the pattern. Saw the side view first. Then saw the front view. Your block will look like this.

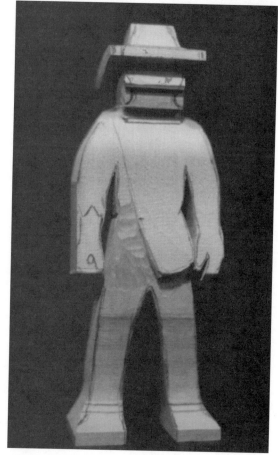

2 With a woodcarving knife, block in the knapsack first. Continue by carving wood away from the right front hip.

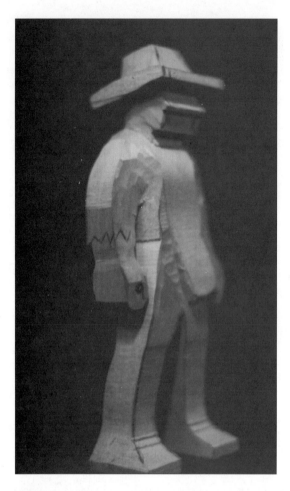

3 Using a pencil, draw on the side view of the arms. Remove any excess wood from around the hands with a carving knife. Use an 8mm shallow gouge to carve the upper shoulder area.

4 Remove wood from the neck and chin area to partially shape the face. Now shape the knapsack to fit the contours of the left hip.

5 Round the crown and the corners of the hat brim. The hat crown is creased lengthwise with a slightly curved brim.

Next, shape the head by first removing wood from each side of the nose. Draw on the eyes, mouth and facial lines. Use a small v-tool to outline the sideburns.

6 Use a 4mm gouge to remove wood from the eye sockets. Leave a small mound of wood in the center of each socket for the eyeball. Next, cut the facial lines with the tip of a knife. Remove the wood below the nose.

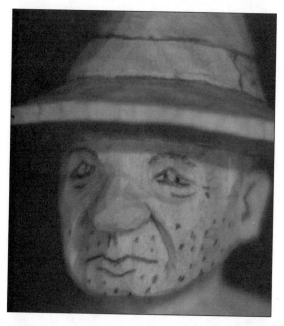

7 Following the pattern, draw the details on the face. Add eyeballs, eyebrows, whiskers and mouth.

8 Carve the details on the face with a woodcarving knife. Use a 6mm v-tool for the lip openings. Wood is removed from the lower lip with a 4mm gouge. Texture the beard with a 3mm v-tool.

 After completing the face and head, follow the general procedures outlined in *Ambush* for rounding the body.

10 Carve the holster separately and attach it after carving the right arm.

11 A back view of the nearly completed carving. All Eagle Eye needs yet is a machete for his hand.

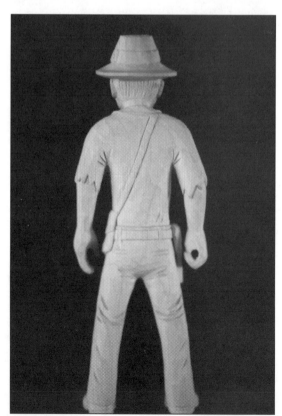

Appendix A
Tools and Materials

Although I now own many fine carving tools, as a boy I began carving with only a pocket knife. While still in high school, I acquired a small six-piece set of carving tools and worked with them for years. They were all I needed to develop the basic skills and fundamentals of wood-carving. My years of past experience has taught me that a few good primary tools and the ability to keep them razor sharp is much more valuable than a chest full of miscellaneous tools that are too dull to cut.

My favorite tools are as listed: a very small awl for punching holes, a good carving knife, a 3mm v-tool, an 8mm v-tool, a 2mm deep gouge, a 4mm deep gouge, a 5mm deep gouge, a 5mm shallow gouge, an 8mm shallow gouge, and a soft Arkansas stone for sharpening.

Linden wood, also called Basswood, is used by a large majority of wood carvers. It is favored most for carving because of its softness and even grain. It has always been my favorite and I use it on all projects, both large and small. However there are other woods that work very well.

If you live in an area where Basswood is not available, I would suggest using #1-grade white pine or sugar pine. Both are suitable for carving and can readily be purchased at most local lumber yards. However, it may be necessary to glue two pieces together to have a block thick enough to accommodate the patterns in this book.

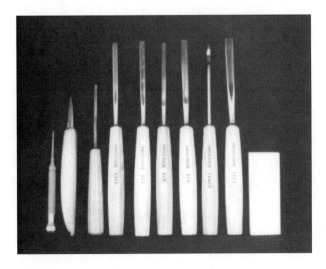

∨ 3mm v-tool

∨ 8mm v-tool

∪ 2mm deep gouge

∪ 4mm deep gouge

∪ 5mm deep gouge

‿ 5mm shallow gouge

‿ 8mm shallow gouge

Jim Maxwell's toolbox includes the following tools (pictured left to right): a very small awl for punching holes, a good carving knife, a 3mm v-tool, an 8mm v-tool, a 2mm deep gouge, a 4mm deep gouge, a 5mm deep gouge, a 5mm shallow gouge, an 8mm shallow gouge, and a soft Arkansas stone. The illustration on the right shows the different cuts for each tool.

Appendix B
Sharpening

The methods of sharpening may differ from one carving instructor to another, however, the importance of sharp tools is equally stressed by all professional carvers. Remember that practice and hands-on experience is the best way to learn how to keep your tools sharp.

While I won't go in to great depth about sharpening here in this book, I do believe it is important to touch on the basics of sharpening.

Sharpening is one of the most important things that a carver must learn. Before your work will take on a fine finished look, you must first learn how to sharpen your tools and keep them sharp. For this you will need a sharpening stone. I prefer a soft Arkansas stone coated with a few drops of honing oil. A fine carborundum or a fine India stone will get equal results.

Lay the knife flat on the stone. Tilt the back of the blade upward about 15-20 degrees and rub the tool across the stone in a circular motion until both sides of the cutting edge become thin and sharp.

Next you must strop the tool to remove any roughness left by the stone. The best method of stropping is to place the knife or tool with the bevel lying flat on the leather strop and pull it backwards across the leather until the bevel becomes polished to a fine razor like edge. I use a white buffing rouge on my strop as it gives an excellent polishing effect.

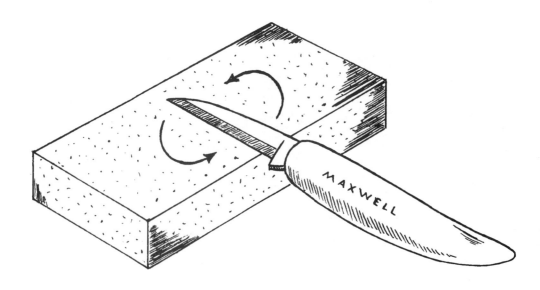

Jim Maxwell prefers to use a soft Arkansas stone coated with a few drops of honing oil to sharpen his tools.

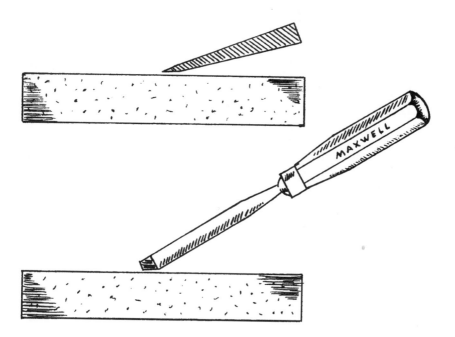

Top: Use a 15-20 degree angle to sharpen knives. Use the stone to sharpen both sides, then strop both sides. Bottom: Use a 30 degree angle to sharpen gouges and v-tools. Use the stone to sharpen the outside bevel only, then strop both sides.

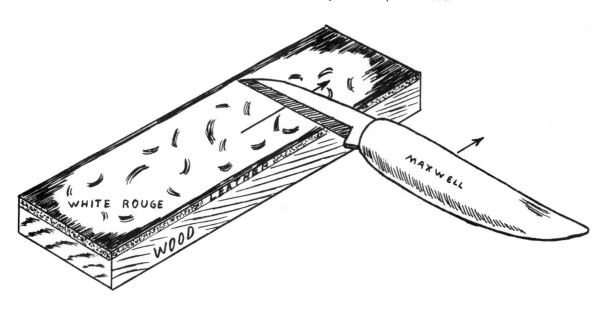

To make a strop, glue a piece of leather to a thin piece of wood. Coat the leather with white buffing rouge. Strop both sides of a knife by pushing the knife backwards away from your body. Then turn the blade over and pull it toward you.

Index

Take a Look at Our Other Fine Woodworking Books

Woodcarving Books by George Lehman

Learn new techniques as you carve these projects designed by professional artists and carver George Lehman. These best-selling books by a master carver are invaluable reference books, PLUS each book contains over 20 ready-to-use patterns.

Book One - Carving Realistic Game and Songbirds - Patterns and instructions
Enthusiastically received by carvers across the US and Canada. George pays particular attention to the needs of beginning carvers in this volume. 20 patterns, over 70 photos, sketches and reference drawing.
ISBN# 1-56523-004-3   96 pages, spiral bound, 14 x 11 inches, includes index, resources $19.95

Book Two - Realism in Wood - 22 projects, detailed patterns and instructions
This volume features a selection of patterns for shorebirds and birds of prey in addition to all-new duck and songbird patterns. Special sections on adding detail, burning.
ISBN# 1-56523-005-1,   112 pages, spiral bound, 14 x 11 inches, includes index, resources $19.95

Book Three - Nature in Wood - patterns for carving 21 smaller birds and 8 wild animals
Focuses on songbirds and small game birds . Numerous tips and techniques throughout including instruction on necessary skills for creating downy feather details and realistic wings. Wonderful section on wild animal carvings with measured patterns.
ISBN #1-56523-006-X   128 pages, soft bound, 11 x 8.5 inches, includes index, resources $16.95

Book Four - Carving Wildlife in Wood- 20 Exciting Projects
Here is George's newest book for decorative woodcarvers with never-before-published patterns. Tremendously detailed, these patterns appeal to carvers at all skill levels. Patterns for birds of prey, ducks, wild turkey, shorebirds and more! Great addition to any carvers library - will be used again and again.
ISBN #1-56523-007-8   96 pages, spiral-bound, 14 x 11 inches, includes index, resources $19.95

Easy to Make Wooden Inlay Projects: Intarsia   by Judy Gale Roberts
Intarsia is a method of making picture mosaics in wood, using a combination of wood grains and colors. The techniques and step-by-step instructions in this book will have you completing your own beautiful pieces in short order. Written by acknowledged expert Judy Gale Roberts, who has her own studio and publishes the Intarsia Times newsletter, produces videos, gives seminars and writes articles on the Intarsia method. Each project is featured in full color and this well written, heavily illustrated features over 100 photographs and includes index and directory of suppliers
ISBN# 56523-023-X   250 pages, soft cover, 8.5 x 11 inches $19.95

Two more great scroll saw books by Judy Gale Roberts! Scroll Saw Fretwork Patterns
Especially designed for the scroll saw enthusiast who wishes to excel, the 'fine line design' method helps you to control drift error found with thick line patterns. Each book features great designs, expert tips, and patterns on oversized (up to 11" x 17" !) sheets in a special "lay flat" spiral binding. Choose the original Design Book 1 with animal and fun designs, or Design Book Two featuring "Western- Southwestern" designs.
Scroll Saw Fretwork Pattern, Design Book One "The Original" $14.95
Scroll Saw Fretwork Patterns, Design Book Two "Western-Southwestern" $16.95

Scroll Saw Woodcrafting Magic! Complete Pattern and How-to Manual   by Joanne Lockwood
Includes complete patterns drawn to scale. You will be amazed at how easy it is to make these beautiful projects when you follow Joanne's helpful tips and work from these clear, precise patterns. Never-before-published patterns for original and creative toys, jewelry, and gifts. Never used a scroll saw? The tutorials in this book will get you started quickly. Experienced scroll-sawers will delight in these all-new, unique projects, perfect for craft sales and gift-giving. Written by Joanne Lockwood, owner of Three Bears Studio in California and the president of the Sacramento Area Woodworkers; she is frequently featured in national woodwork and craft magazines.
ISBN# 1-56523-024-8   180 pages, soft cover, 8.5 x 11 inches $14.95

Making Signs in Wood with Your Router   by Paul Merrills
I f you own a router, you can produce beautiful personalized signs and designs easily and inexpensively. This is the complete manual for beginners and professionals. Features over 100 clear photos, easy-to-follow instructions, ready-to-use designs, and six complete sign making alphabets. Techniques range from small nameplates to world-class showpieces trimmed with gold leaf.
ISBN# 56523-026-4 250 pages, 8.5 x 11 inches; includes index and suppliers directory $19.95

- -

To order: If you can't find these at your favorite bookseller you may order direct from the publisher
at the prices listed above plus $2.00 per book shipping.
Send check or money order to:

Fox Chapel Publishing
Box 7948D
Lancaster, Pennsylvania , 17604

You are invited to Join the

National Wood Carvers Association

" Some carve their careers: others just chisel"
<u>since 1953</u>

If you have any interest in woodcarving: if you carve wood , create wood sculpture or even just whittle in your spare time , you will enjoy your membership in the National Wood Carvers Association. The non-profit NWCA is the world's largest carving club with over 33,000 members. There are NWCA members in more than 56 countries around the globe.

The Association's goals are to:

* promote wood carving
* foster fellowship among member enthusiasts
* encourage exhibitions and area get togethers
* list sources of equipment and information for the
   wood carving artist
* provide a forum for carving artists

The NWCA serves as a valuable network of tips, hints and helpful information for the wood carver. Membership is only $8.00 per year.

Members receive the magazine "Chip Chats" six times a year, free with their membership. "Chip Chats" contains articles, news events, demonstrations of technique, patterns and a full color section showcasing examples of fine craftsmanship. Through this magazine you will be kept up to date on shows and workshops to attend, new products , special offers to NWCA members and other members' activities in you area and around the world.

National Wood Carvers Association
7424 Miami Ave.,
Cincinnati, Ohio 45243

Name:_____

Address:_____

Dues $8.00 per year in USA , $10.00 per year foreign (payable in US Funds)